A

GUIDE

TO

PLATO'S

REPUBLIC

A
GUIDE
TO
PLATO'S
REPUBLIC

—⚏—

Daryl H. Rice

New York   Oxford
OXFORD UNIVERSITY PRESS
1998

Oxford University Press

Oxford New York
Athens Auckland Bangkok Bogota Bombay Buenos Aires
Calcutta Cape Town Dar es Salaam Delhi Florence Hong Kong
Istanbul Karachi Kuala Lumpur Madras Madrid Melbourne
Mexico City Nairobi Paris Singapore Taipei Tokyo Toronto

and associated companies in
Berlin Ibadan

Copyright © 1998 by Oxford University Press, Inc.

Published by Oxford University Press, Inc.
198 Madison Avenue, New York, New York 10016

Oxford is a registered trademark of Oxford University Press

Library of Congress Cataloging-in-Publication Data
Rice, Daryl H., 1952-
A guide to Plato's Republic / Daryl H. Rice.
p.   cm.
Includes bibliographical references and index.
ISBN 0-19-511283-0 (cloth: alk. paper) —
ISBN 0-19-511284-9 (pbk.: alk. paper)
1. Plato. Republic. 2. Political science—Early works to 1800.
3. Utopias. I. Title.
JC71.P6R47 1998   96-43917
321'.07—dc20   CIP

1 3 5 7 9 8 6 4 2

Printed in the United States of America
on acid-free paper

Knowledge for the sake of knowledge is, say what you will, nothing but a dismal begging of the question. . . . While men believe themselves to be seeking truth for its own sake, they are in fact seeking life in truth.

—Miguel de Unamuno, *Tragic Sense of Life*

Contents

Preface

USING THIS BOOK

As an interpretive guide, this brief volume is no substitute for the *Republic* itself. It is not even a comprehensive commentary. I analyze many of Plato's arguments in some detail and provide periodic summaries in which I gather them up to show their place in the overarching plan of the *Republic*, but since I only allude to other arguments, you do yourself a grave disservice if you do not read the original text. Even to get a basic understanding of the interpretive arguments offered here you will need to be familiar with Plato's exposition.

More important, if you do not read the *Republic*, you deprive yourself of the means for keeping me honest. One way to approach this book is as a particular case study in the art of interpretation; it is *an* interpretation that I offer here, not the only one possible. I am more interested in your learning generally how interpretations are put together and how one goes about making a case for them than I am in convincing you of my particular interpretation of the *Republic*.

This is not to say I think all interpretations are equally plausible. If I believed that, I could not muster the energy to construct my own; but I recognize that I might have erred, and only if you read the *Republic* for yourself will you be in a position to decide if I have. Although I note alternative interpretations at various places throughout the book, I can only give my own account of the views I reject. It is up to you to give yourself every possible advantage for judging whether the interpretive options I pursue earn their keep.

If you are reading the *Republic* for a course, your teacher may assign only selected portions of the text. I have done so myself in classes where I teach texts in addition to the *Republic*. Going this route is inevitably to miss some rich detail, but it will do in a pinch. You need not read the *Republic* in its entirety to learn from this book, but the more of Plato's text you can get under your belt, the greater the benefits will be.

As a general introduction to philosophy and political theory, the present volume is motivated by several pedagogical assumptions and convictions. I assume that you have some interest in actually doing a bit of theorizing and philosophizing, that you want to do more than learn a few names and ideas that you can drop to impress people at parties. If you are interested in articulating and systematizing your own philosophical and political beliefs, you could, of course, lock yourself in a room and compose a list of your beliefs. I suspect, however, that upon emerging to find others criticizing you for having ignored some dimension of politics or life, or for having listed beliefs that on closer inspection turn out to be contradictory, you would soon find the project a rather daunting task. Indeed, you might feel intellectually paralyzed.

An alternative is to recognize that one need not completely reinvent the wheel; you are not unique in that many others before you have probably held similar beliefs. Reading other philosophers and political theorists can be a more efficient way of going about things. Not that you are going to find a philosopher or theorist with whom you agree on all points, but you can use other thinkers as foils for considering the complexity of your own beliefs and their interrelations. Even if you are so mechanical when reading another thinker as to mark an *X* by all propositions with which you agree and an *O* by those with which you disagree, you will go a long way toward illuminating and systematizing your own ideas.

The greater the number of other theorists and philosophers you read, the richer your own thinking will be. My experience as a student and teacher, however, have convinced me that, at the introductory level, sustained reflection on a few texts of a few thinkers is the most effective way to learn how the enterprises of philosophy and political theory go about their business. The advantage of this approach is that it teaches you how to impose discipline on your thinking. You see the difficulty and importance of getting the pieces to fit together as a whole. Theorizing about politics and philosophy is sometimes like punching a pillow; you get rid of a lump only to find it reappear in another place. It is easier to learn how to think systematically by studying a particular extensive example of systematic thought than by reading about various thinkers in a textbook or reading short excerpts from the works of those thinkers.

There are many texts on which you could cut your theoretical and philosophical teeth. I do not want to argue too long or loudly for the superiority of my choice of Plato's *Republic*. I confess, though, that I write this book in the spirit of Alfred North Whitehead, a twentieth-century philosopher who once quipped that the whole of western philosophy is but a "series of footnotes" to Plato. Whitehead did not mean that Plato raised and successfully answered all the relevant questions; rather, he meant that Plato roughly marked out the territory within which subsequent western philosophy would operate, and raised at least some of the bigger questions it would address. You can disagree vehemently with Plato's answers to the questions he raised, and even argue that he posed the wrong questions, Whitehead suggests, but Plato's thought stands as a touchstone against which much of subsequent philosophy must define itself, either positively or negatively.

In studying the *Republic* we can learn not only about Plato's particular philosophy and political theory but a great deal about philosophy and political theory in general. I use my running interpretation of the *Republic*, then, as an opportunity to introduce you to some of the problems with which philosophy and political theory are still grappling, to some of the approaches that have been taken toward resolving those problems, and to some of the technical terminology employed in such approaches. In other words, I sometimes go off on tangents from the *Republic*. Although this plan assumes that Plato is still relevant today, it does not assume that he thought the way most moderns do. In fact, Plato is particularly useful as a foil against which we can become more aware of our own beliefs and their implications because he provides such a contrast to many of our own beliefs.

The *Republic* has been divided by scholars into ten "Books," or what we would call chapters. My own discussion does not always strictly follow Plato's order of exposition. While commenting on an earlier section of the text, I sometimes refer to arguments that Plato makes in a later section and vice versa. For the most part, however, my own chapters correspond roughly to Plato's Books, or blocks of Books, in the order in which they appear in the *Republic*. Thus, you need not read the whole *Republic* before consulting this work; you can read the Books of the *Republic* noted after each chapter title and then read the chapter before proceeding to read more of Plato.

Although I compare Plato's position on various matters with other views, and contrast my own interpretive positions with alternative ones, I do not always mention in the main text the names of thinkers espousing such alternatives. Instead, I refer you to these persons and their works in a short list of suggestions for further reading at the end of every chapter. The amount of material written about Plato and the *Republic* is staggering in volume; even small libraries are likely to have several shelves of books, and this does not take into account the seemingly endless number of articles published in scholarly journals. What is important at this point is that you go head to head with Plato himself. Should you get more interested Plato or other thinkers — and I hope I can spark such an interest — you can easily get a start on compiling a more comprehensive bibliography by consulting the books that I mention in the suggestions for further reading. (I indicate only authors and titles in the suggestions. For complete bibliographical information, consult the select bibliography at the back of the book, where the works are arranged alphabetically by author.)

Inability to pronounce words in a text makes reading difficult and needlessly inhibits discussion of the text. Accordingly, I have placed at the beginning of the book a guide to pronouncing the names of the main characters in the *Republic* and a few other Greeks names and terms that have been transliterated into English (these are words originally spelled in the Greek alphabet that have been translated into the English alphabet). Once you learn the rhythm of their pronunciation — where the primary stress, or accent, falls — you will be able to take a pretty good stab at pronouncing names and terms that are not in the guide.

I use G. M. A. Grube's translation of the *Republic*. Many other translations, however, such as those by Bloom, Cornford, Jowett, Lee, Rouse, or Waterfield, will also do. Many of these are available in paperback. (See the entries under these names in the select bibliography at the back of this book for complete bibliographical information.) Although differences between translations might be important for advanced scholarly work on matters of fine detail, none of my arguments is so narrowly based that it would be invalidated by a reputable alternative translation.

I do recommend that you read an edition that includes the Stephanus system of pagination. Since Plato did not number the lines or paragraphs of the *Republic*, it would be difficult for scholars working from different Greek editions — or from translations in different languages and from different translations in the same language — to direct readers to specific passages without some commonly recognized system for doing so. Fortunately there is such a system. The Stephanus family, an old line of European printers and scholars, divided their edition of Plato's collected works into numbered sections — the *Republic* running from sections 327 to 621 — and lettered the subsections *a* through *e*. I abide by this convention. Thus, a reference to 357c, for example, is a reference to section 357, subsection c, in the Stephanus system. Some editions include this "pagination" in the margins, while others only note at the top of each page what sections identified by the Stephanus system are included on that page. So long as you read an edition of either type, you should be able to quickly locate the specific passages to which I refer.

ACKNOWLEDGMENTS

I am in debt to all my students who have demanded that I give intelligible responses to their questions about the *Republic*, but a special thank you goes to Lisa Caldwell and Shane Knight, who gave me extensive written comments on an early draft of the manuscript. My treatment of Plato's doctrine of the tripartite soul began as a response I wrote to a draft of George Klosko's *The Development of Plato's Political Theory* (Methuen, 1986) when I was Klosko's graduate assistant. We still do not agree, but the spirited conversations we had then helped shape the account I give here. Michael Puntney read the entire manuscript and urged me to make it more readable in many places. Ed Anson and Sandra Dwyer offered suggestions about the guide to pronunciation. The anonymous referees for Oxford University Press will still disagree with me on some matters, but their criticisms helped to make the book much better than it otherwise would have been. I thank Robert Miller of Oxford University Press for his initial interest in yet another book about the *Republic*. Liam Dalzell, his assistant, was always ready with prompt and knowledgeable responses to queries about final manuscript preparation. Martha Morss, the copyeditor, significantly improved the readability of the text, and John Bauco, project editor, coordinated production with a keen eye for detail. Finally, a special word of gratitude to Michael Weinstein, who read the entire manuscript and made invaluable suggestions throughout. My debt is for more than that, though: He taught me how to think and teach by exemplifying what living philosophy is all about.

Little Rock, Arkansas   D. H. R.
March 1997

Guide to Pronunciation

Disagreement abounds about how to pronounce Greek names and terms transliterated into English. I do not want to contribute to those disputes. The following simple guide to a few names and terms yields pronunciations that are common. I have included the names of the main characters in the *Republic* along with a few other names and terms that appear in chapters to follow. When you say each word, stress the syllable that appears in capital letters.

Adeimantus:	ah-die-MAHN-tus
aretē:	ar-rah-TAY
Aristotle:	ar-uh-STOT-l or AR-uh-stot-l
Aristophanes:	ar-uh-STOFF-uh-neez
ergon:	ER-gone
Cephalus:	SEF-uh-lus or KEF-uh-lus
Glaucon:	GLAW-con
Homer:	HOE-mer
Parmenides:	par-MEN-uh-deez
Piraeus:	pie-REE-us
Plato:	PLAY-toe
Polemarchus:	pall-uh-MARK-us
Simonides:	sigh-MAHN-uh-deez
Socrates:	SOCK-ruh-teez
Thrasymachus:	thrah-SIM-uh-cus
nomos:	NO-mos
Xenophon:	ZEN-eh-fun

A

GUIDE

TO

PLATO'S

REPUBLIC

1

Philosophy and
Ordinary Life: Book I

PLATO'S DIALOGICAL STYLE

The first questions I usually hear from students about the *Republic*
concern its style: Since the *Republic* is a work of philosophy and
political theory, why does Plato present it as a conversation among
friends? Why does he bother to put his arguments into the mouths
of a cast of characters rather than just state what he has to say in a
straightforward manner? We know, after all, that it is Plato who is
determining the speeches that his characters make, so why all the
drama? Students often see the dramatic, or dialogical, form as disin-
genuous. They protest that although Plato portrays his conclusions
as the result of a genuine debate among equals, he knows in
advance where he wants to go and constructs the dialogue so that
his views, put into the mouth of Socrates, always win out. Socrates is
self-effacing and fawns and bows before the supposed brilliance of
the other participants in the conversation, but their arguments are

1

really just straw men concocted so that Socrates can blow them apart with ease.

There are no easy or noncontroversial ways of responding to this objection. Most commentators on the *Republic* contend that Plato's choice of the dialogical style is significant, and some argue that it is even the primary key to understanding the content of the work. I will return later in this chapter to a fuller discussion of these complexities. For now I suggest that we interpret Plato's choice of a dramatic style as an attempt to show the place of philosophy in life. While this interpretation may not always reflect Plato's explicit intentions, it does allow us to mine some valuable insights about the general character of philosophy.

The *Republic* opens with a description of people going about the ordinary business of their lives (327a–331d). Socrates has gone down to the Piraeus (the port of Athens) to pray and to watch a religious festival. On returning to the main part of the city, he encounters some friends, who convince him to come home with them to bide the time before going to see another festival that evening. The conversation at first is rambling and casual and punctuated with chitchat. Cephalus, the father in the household to which they have retired, comments on his old age and its consequences. In the course of responding to Socrates' question as to how wealth might make old age easier, Cephalus remarks that with death approaching he has begun to worry more about whether he has been unjust to anyone during his life. Wealth, he says, will at least allow him to depart this life without fear of having been unjust to anyone in the sense of not having paid them back what he owed them. Socrates picks up on this conception of justice and asks whether it is really adequate. The dialogue is then off and running in pursuit of the question that organizes the rest of the work: What is justice?

Plato could have made that question the first sentence of the work, so why the dillydallying around? While you may find his approach to be contrived, Plato's warm-up to the question of justice helps to demystify philosophy by showing that philosophical questions emerge in the ordinary course of life. The question of justice arises, not among professors practicing some arcane academic discipline divorced from life, but among people very much engaged with life. The dramatic form of Plato's presentation makes the point that for all human beings life consists of both action and reflection on the problems related to action. Philosophy develops the reflective component of life into an art form with its own specialized vocabulary and history (philosophers are always referring to the work of other, previous philosophers). This can make philosophy seem far removed from ordinary life, but the questions it addresses are at bottom rooted in this life. Philosophy grows out of life and can be seen as an attempt to give a comprehensive account of life and its complexities.

The whole thrust of Book I, the content as well as the dialogical form, is more about the general character of philosophy than justice per se. Once the topic of justice comes up, seemingly accidentally in the course of casual conversation, Plato has the characters run through a slew of arguments about it and arrive at some conclusions: Justice is not a matter of returning what is owed (at least, not in any simplistic or unqualified sense); justice is not a matter of helping friends and harming enemies; justice is not the advantage of the stronger; a just ruler works for the advantage of the ruled; justice is virtue — good and wise; and the just person will live a happier and more profitable life. These are all conclusions for which Socrates argues, yet he confesses at the end of Book I that they all strike him as rather empty (354b). Since he has not discovered what justice itself is, he cannot be sure his statements about its relations to virtue, goodness, wisdom, happiness, and so forth are valid. How can one know what a thing's relation to something else is unless one knows what the thing itself is? "Hence the result of the discussion, as far as I'm concerned," he laments, "is that I know nothing."

Although Plato has Socrates introduce in a provisional way some points about justice that he will pick up later on, many of the arguments concerning justice have a peculiar negative quality; they seem to be more about what justice is not than what it is. Socrates seems more interested in shaking his friends' confidence in their views of justice than he is in putting forward a conception of his own at this point. Polemarchus, for example, tries to defend the claim that justice is helping friends and harming enemies (331d–334b). When

Socrates leads Polemarchus to see that according to this conception stealing would be just so long as it is done to help friends and harm enemies, and then asks Polemarchus if this is really what he means, the frustrated Polemarchus exclaims, "No, by God, it isn't. I don't know any more what I did mean. . . ."

The confession of confusion and ignorance is perhaps more important than the details of the arguments that provoke it. By the time Plato sat down to write the *Republic*, he had already spent a great deal of time reflecting on justice and many other topics — philosophizing, that is — and he felt he had something to offer on these matters that was superior to the run-of-the-mill pronouncements he heard in daily conversation. His readers, though, must have a motivation for listening to him; they will be receptive to what he has to say only if they acknowledge doubts about what they already believe. Plato has to create room for what he thinks to be his own, better conceptions by first clearing the ground of some other, inferior ideas.

THE SOCIOLOGY OF KNOWLEDGE
AND QUESTIONING AUTHORITY

If philosophizing begins in casual conversation about ordinary life, what does Plato believe to be inadequate in casual conversation? What in casual conversation propels it toward the more rigorous and systematic effort that we call philosophy? Plato seems to be trying to demonstrate that philosophy not only originates in ordinary life but that it is necessary to ordinary life, at least if we are to be confident that we really know anything about life.

Recall once more how the first conception of justice arises (330d–331d). In talking about the advantages of wealth in old age, Cephalus implies that justice is returning what one owes. When Socrates challenges this by suggesting that it surely would not be just to return a weapon to a person who has gone insane, Cephalus quickly caves in. He remarks that what Socrates says is true and then departs, never to be heard from in the dialogue again. Cephalus's son, Polemarchus, is not so quick to capitulate to Socrates; he believes his father's conception of justice is correct and takes up its defense. One gets the impression that Polemarchus knows that his father did not really change his mind, that he was just not interested in pursuing the question further and only agreed with Socrates as a polite way of excusing himself from the conversation.

What is the source of Polemarchus's confidence in his view of justice? One possible explanation is simply that he inherited the view from his father. To use modern jargon, our beliefs are often the product of our socialization, and as sociologists and psychologists point out, the most potent influence on socialization is the family. Polemarchus is reflective enough, however, to recognize that the influence of socialization is quite broad; although our views might derive most directly from our parents, their views, in turn, are rooted in a much larger culture. So, in defending justice as returning what is owed, he immediately remarks — seeming to believe it bolsters his case — that his view is also held by Simonides, a well-known Greek poet (331d). Socrates later notes other famous persons who also hold this view of justice, including Homer, the most famous of Greek poets (334a–b, 335d–336a). However, Socrates prods Polemarchus into questioning these supposed authorities, the poets, whose influence then may have been as powerful in shaping public opinion as the influence of the mass media is in our own day. If we recognize that many of our views are not our own inventions, and are often traceable to so-called authorities, the question arises whether the views of the purported authorities are actually correct.

Polemarchus does not raise this question. Nor does Socrates in an overt way; but it is the question that motivates his interrogation of Polemarchus, for by the end of their discussion he has Polemarchus questioning commonly recognized authority figures as a valid source of support for his position. After Polemarchus first drags the opinion of Simonides into the argument, Socrates agrees, rather sarcastically, that Simonides is "a wise and godlike man," but adds immediately that he has no idea on earth what the man means (331e). When Polemarchus attempts to clarify what Simonides might mean, he gradually works around (with Socrates' help, of course) to the conclusion that he must mean that justice is helping friends and harming enemies.

Socrates, as we know, rips into this claim as well and gets Pole-marchus to agree that it is false. He not only gets Polemarchus to question the authority of so-called authority figures, but he offers an explanation for why these figures might hold the conception of jus-tice that they do: they are (or were) all rich men who have the finan-cial means to always succeed in helping their friends and harming their enemies (336a). Their conception of justice very conveniently fits the way they actually live their lives.

Here Plato has Socrates practice what, in modern parlance, is called the sociology of knowledge. One can go about investigating any claim to knowledge in several general ways. One way is to disre-gard who holds the view; the sole question is whether the claim is true, regardless of who espouses it. In this book, for example, I am usually more interested in examining the validity of the arguments in the *Republic* than I am in the fact that it was Plato who made them. Another way to test a claim to knowledge is to investigate the rela-tion between what is said and who said it; this approach is based on the sociology of knowledge. One tries to explain why those who hold a view might easily believe it to be true given their position in society. For example, those who enjoy privileged roles in society might hold views, perhaps quite unconsciously, that legitimize the status quo; according to these views things are just as they should be. Those on the lower end of the social ladder may hold views that challenge the status quo and legitimize attempts to change the way things are.

Sociologies of knowledge can be developed into highly complex accounts of why people believe what they believe, but the basic idea is simple. As I am writing this chapter, spokespersons for Amer-ican cigarette companies, some with scientific credentials, are claim-ing that cigarette smoking is not addictive and does not cause cancer. I suspect that persons other than just philosophers are won-dering whether what is being said has some connection to who is saying it (although in this situation the connection may be more self-conscious and cynical than is often the case). Carried to an extreme, the sociology of knowledge seems to say that any claim to knowledge is tainted by the social interests of those making it. It would be difficult, however, to avoid the sociology of knowledge altogether. We have all accused a person of saying something because it protects his or her own interests. The underlying idea is that we cannot always take what people say at face value. To this the sociology of knowledge only adds the further idea that, when interests and knowledge are related, an individual's interests are rarely unique and are often shared by others in similar social positions.

While the sociology of knowledge does not necessarily invalidate all claims to knowledge, it does raise troublesome questions. Which of the pronouncements we make in casual conversation are really true, and which do we believe to be true because they fit with our self-interests? Of those views we inherit from commonly recognized authorities, which are really true, and which are believed to be true by the so-called authorities because of their own social positions? By bringing Polemarchus to the point of questioning whether recognized authorities are a reliable source of confidence in his beliefs, Socrates has taken him a long way toward recognizing the need for more sustained reflection on what he thinks he knows.

APPEARANCE AND REALITY AND QUESTIONING COMMON SENSE

But maybe Polemarchus is too gullible in being swayed to think that ordinary life is fraught with problems that point toward the need for philosophy. The character Thrasymachus certainly thinks so. Just after Socrates has concluded his conversation with Polemarchus, Thrasymachus explodes into the dialogue — impatient, exasperated, fed up with what he thinks is a lot of hot air (336b-339a). Things really are not as difficult as Socrates makes them out to be. If Socrates would stop with the word games and call a spade a spade, he might make some headway instead of spinning his wheels and going in circles. There is no need for special, fanciful philosophical reflection to figure out what justice is; anybody with two cents worth of wits and a little common sense can see what it is. In any society there are those who rule (the strongest) and those who are ruled. Those who rule do so by making and enforcing laws. Justice is obedience to those laws and injustice is disobedience to them. Since those who make the laws are not fools, and since they make laws that work to their own advantage, justice turns out to be the advantage of the strongest. End of discussion.

Socrates reports being taken aback by this outburst, but Plato probably exaggerates the surprise. Socrates had heard this sort of view before. In fact, before you jump to the conclusion that Plato uses only straw men, or caricatures of real persons who espouse weak arguments, in his dialogue, I suggest you attend closely to the character of Thrasymachus. (I have found him to be pretty representative of many persons sitting in my classroom.) If Socrates cannot convince people like Thrasymachus of the need for philosophy, he is going to be left with a pretty small audience for the rest of the dialogue. Socrates' response to Thrasymachus is aimed at getting him, too, to make the general admission that things are not always as simple as they seem.

If Socrates can wring such an admission from Thrasymachus, he will at least open the way for philosophical thinking, for at the core of every fully developed philosophy is a distinction between appearance and reality. If philosophy, generally defined, is the attempt to give a comprehensive account of life with all its complexities, a philosopher, in effect, makes a declaration that such and such is the way things really are. Others may disagree: "Oh yeah? It certainly is not obvious that things are such and such. In fact, it seems to us that things are not such and such but are rather so and so."

If the philosopher is a good one, he or she must take account of these objections. If things are *really* such and such, why do they at least *appear* to some persons to be so and so? And the explanation of why things can appear to be other than what they really are must itself be based on the way things really are. That is, the philosopher must build into his or her general account of the way things really are an explanation of how their complexity makes it possible for them to appear to be other than what they really are.

Any critic of a particular philosophy must abide by the same requirement. He or she must explain how, if things are really so and so (rather than such and such, as the first philosopher claims), it is possible for them to appear to be such and such. We can view the history of philosophy as a long debate about appearance and reality; what one philosopher declares is real, another philosopher claims is only appearance, and vice versa.

In talking about how philosophy operates, I have already waxed rather philosophical. And it is just this sort of discussion with which Thrasymachus seems so impatient. Socrates' strategy, however, is directed at showing that as thorny as the distinction between appearance and reality might be, even Thrasymachus employs it in his supposedly down-to-earth views. If Socrates can succeed in doing this, he disarms Thrasymachus's protest that philosophy is a worthless enterprise.

Socrates has already invoked the distinction between appearance and reality in his discussion with Polemarchus, when he asked Polemarchus what he meant by "friends and enemies" in saying that justice is helping friends and harming enemies: "Speaking of friends, do you mean those a person *believes* to be good and useful to him or those who *actually are* good and useful, even if he doesn't think they are, and similarly with enemies?" (334c; emphasis added). Do human beings sometimes make mistakes, he asks, about who are really their friends and who their enemies? Socrates uses a similar strategy in arguing against Thrasymachus's statement that justice is the advantage of the strongest (339a–e). Thrasymachus says rulers make laws that, if obeyed by the ruled, work to the advantage of the rulers. But Socrates gets Thrasymachus to admit that rulers sometimes make mistakes, that they sometimes make laws that seem to be to their advantage but that really are not. Obedience to such laws by the ruled actually works to the disadvantage of the rulers.

Although Socrates introduces the distinction between appearance and reality, Thrasymachus uses it himself to try to get out of the corner into which Socrates has pushed him (340c–d). He protests that he wants to clarify what he means by a ruler. By ruler, he says, he means a true ruler, and not just one who seems to be a ruler. A real ruler would never make mistakes. The debate then turns to a further discussion of what a real ruler is. Do real rulers rule for their own advantage, as Thrasymachus asserts, or for the advantage of the ruled? Socrates takes the latter position and seems to win the day. However, Socrates' most important triumph is not in winning the debate but in forcing Thrasymachus to see the necessity of resorting to a level of discourse that recognizes the distinction between appearance and reality, and thus presupposes that things are not as simple as Thrasymachus suggested in his initial outburst.

When Thrasymachus first bursts into the conversation, he objects to Socrates' method of nit-picking another person's definition of a concept (336b–d). The meaning of a concept is not all that complicated, he seems to imply; if we relied on a little common sense, we would not get entangled in all the ponderous problems that Socrates' method of philosophizing creates. Yet Thrasymachus later undermines his own stance (340d). When trying to clarify what he means when he says that a true ruler would not make mistakes, he compares a ruler to a doctor, an accountant, and a grammarian. Would you call a person a doctor when he makes a mistake in diagnosing a patient, he asks? Would you call someone who makes mistakes in mathematical calculations an accountant, or someone who does not properly diagram a sentence a grammarian? To be sure, he admits, "I think that we express ourselves in words that, taken literally, do say that a doctor is in error, or an accountant, or a grammarian." But if we give a "precise account" of matters, Thrasymachus continues, we should not say these things. If we think about things more closely — if we go beyond our unreflective, habitual, and casual way of expressing things and instead use words more carefully — we see that we define a real doctor precisely as one who correctly diagnoses illnesses. Persons who do not diagnose illnesses correctly may be quacks, carpenters, or a lot of other things, but they are not real doctors.

Socrates is only too eager to speak precisely, as we know, and goes on to beat Thrasymachus at his own game. He argues that just as real doctors practice the art of medicine for the benefit of patients' bodies rather than for their own advantage, real rulers practice the art of ruling for the benefit of the ruled rather than for their own advantage (341c–342e). Again, however, Socrates' apparent victory is not as important in itself as his success in getting Thrasymachus to accept the terms under which the game must be played, that is, the use of precise speech.

Thrasymachus admits, in effect, that so-called common sense cannot function as any final court of appeal in determining what is appearance and what is reality. We sometimes triumphantly declare our position in an argument to be correct because "it's just plain common sense." But what do we do when our opponent claims the same advantage for his or her own position? One person's common sense can be outrageous stupidity to another person. And we can hardly appeal to common sense to settle a dispute about what common sense is. Common sense is only a rough-and-ready way we express ourselves, as Thrasymachus might put it. It is a workaday distillation of what by habit, custom, and convention we believe to be true. This kind of knowledge may be common in that it is widely shared or held by many—indeed, if it were not, it would not get us by as often as it does—but *widely shared* is not the same as *universally shared*. Our habitual, customary, and conventional ways of thinking are not always the same, and when we encounter these differences the inadequacy of common sense as a court of appeal becomes apparent. The twentieth-century philosopher Alfred North Whitehead argues that philosophy can be defined, in part, as the critic of common sense. Our habitual and customary ways of viewing things can hardly be a complete web of lies, he argues, but neither can they function as an obvious standard of truth. So-called common sense is sometimes the problem rather than the solution. Plato makes a similar point by having Thrasymachus recognize the inadequacy of our usual manner of speaking.

NORMATIVE PHILOSOPHY
VERSUS EMPIRICAL INQUIRY

Plato also wants to undermine another, specific claim that Thrasymachus makes in his initial tirade. Thrasymachus equates justice with legality and, in so doing, seems to assert the superiority of a hard-nosed realism over airy philosophical speculation. If whatever is legal is just and whatever is illegal is unjust, then it would be non-sensical to inquire about the justice of the laws themselves. That is, if justice is defined at the outset as whatever is legal, then to ask about the justice of the laws themselves would be like asking if the laws are legal, which would be silly. Under Thrasymachus's formula, a question that clearly interests Socrates cannot even be asked in a meaningful way.

Allow me to frame the situation here in contemporary terms. Many modern philosophers and social scientists draw a distinction between *empirical* and *normative* inquiry. Empirical inquiry seeks to determine what the facts are, pure and simple, without making any value judgements, that is, without saying whether the facts are good or bad, just or unjust, fair or unfair, moral or immoral. This sort of inquiry is practiced by natural scientists. If your chemistry professor concluded a lecture on the composition of water by saying that he or she found it grossly unfair or immoral that each molecule of water should have only one atom of oxygen for every two atoms of hydro-gen, you would probably enroll in another section of the course! You would do so, not because you think that the composition of water is fair and moral, but because you think morality and fairness have noth-ing to do with the facts of the molecular structure of water.

Normative inquiry, on the other hand, seeks to determine what *ought* to be or what *should* be in a moral or ethical sense. It is con-cerned not with facts but with values (and thus the empirical/nor-mative distinction is often referred to as the fact/value distinction). Normative statements or theories always include some value judg-ment. For example, when social theorists assert that modern liberal democracies are superior to feudal societies, in which privileges were inherited through birth, they are not simply describing the facts of feudal and liberal democratic societies but rendering a value judgment on those facts. Both kinds of societies have existed in fact, but the theorist is declaring that if a society is to be fair and just, then it ought to be organized along liberal democratic lines.

Plato is obviously interested in what we would call normative inquiry; he wants to determine how societies ought to be organized if they are to be just, rather than merely describe societies as they have existed in fact. To do this he must first determine what justice is. But if justice is equivalent to legality, as Thrasymachus says, the only worthwhile enterprise would be to examine empirically what the laws in fact permit and prohibit. Plato's pursuit would not only be useless but meaningless.

I find Thrasymachus's protest interesting because I have had many students who, two or three weeks into a political-theory course, express a similar exasperation: "What these political philosophers say is all very nice. Justice is this and not that. A fair society would be so and so. Wonderful. But none of it amounts to a hill of beans in the real world. Are we ever going to get down to the nitty-gritty and talk about the way things actually work?" The whole enterprise of rigorous normative inquiry strikes them as odd if not completely futile.

What Plato shows through Thrasymachus is that the attempt to *avoid* normative discourse is futile; those who try to consistently maintain such a stance are doomed to trip over themselves sooner or later. When Thrasymachus's equation of justice and legality is challenged, he makes increasingly cynical statements in order to defend it, finally declaring that injustice is actually virtue (348b–349a). Thrasymachus's reasoning seems to be this: Since rulers make laws to their own advantage, justice is the advantage of the rulers, or the strongest. What, then, about the ruled? If the laws are rigged to the advantage of the rulers, then obedience to the laws (justice, according to Thrasymachus) by the ruled would work to their disadvantage. If the ruled are just, they are not going to live very full, happy or profitable lives; indeed, for the ruled, injustice (disobedience to the laws) would be virtue, and justice (obedience to the laws) vice. This line of argument presupposes, of course, that the persons under discussion are those who can be unjust in a big way, who can disobey the law and get away with it, rather than two-bit burglars or kidnappers who get caught. In fact, Thrasymachus says, it is tyrants—who are so lawless that they disobey the established law about who is to make laws, subjugate entire cities to themselves, and change their own edicts at whim—who profit the most from injustice (343a–344c, 348d).

Thrasymachus does not succeed, however, in escaping a consideration of what is good and what is bad in a normative sense; he only inverts completely what most other people believe to be good and bad. Socrates sees the position into which Thrasymachus has worked himself and believes he can demonstrate its untenability, so he asks Thrasymachus if he is serious in saying that injustice is virtue: "If you had declared that injustice is more profitable, but agreed that it is a vice or shameful, as some others do, we could have discussed the matter on the basis of conventional beliefs" (348e–349a). Look, Socrates seems to say, many persons might argue that disobedience to the laws (at least when one can get away with it) would be more profitable than obeying the laws, but they would not confuse profit with virtue. They might counsel in favor of pursuing what is profitable, but they would still recognize that there is something shameful about doing so. At least they would not go so far as to call living in disobedience to the laws virtue. But you, Thrasymachus, seem to being saying something more. If I understand you correctly, you actually want to call injustice good, "to include it with virtue and wisdom." Thrasymachus replies that Socrates understands him perfectly.

Thrasymachus apparently did not really agree to the conclusion of the prior argument that a real ruler would make laws advantageous to the ruled. The reasoning behind his statement that injustice is virtue still presupposes that real rulers make laws to their own advantage. Thus, Socrates could have defeated Thrasymachus's assertion that injustice is virtue by holding him to the conclusion of the earlier argument about what a real ruler is and drawing out its implication. If the conclusion of the earlier argument holds, then, contrary to what Thrasymachus says, obedience to the laws on the part of the ruled would allow them to lead full, happy, and profitable lives. That is, Socrates could show that if real rulers make laws to the advantage of the ruled, and if justice is merely obedience to the laws, then justice would be a virtue for the ruled. Socrates does not press this argument, though, since it buys into the equation of justice and legality (the second premise), which is the root of the problem in Thrasymachus's position. To win the argument that justice is virtue by accepting this premise would be to win the battle but lose the war.

So Socrates takes another, more indirect tack (349b–350d). He allows Thrasymachus to assume that justice is legality and that rulers make laws to their own advantage, and he attacks the proposition that Thrasymachus believes these underlying assumptions produce — injustice is virtue — from another angle. Socrates first gets Thrasymachus to add a few additional statements to his claim that injustice is virtue and then mounts what is called a *reductio ad absurdum* argument against the whole group of statements; he attempts to reduce Thrasymachus's position to an obvious absurdity.

Arguments of this type work as follows. First, one gets the opponent to state his or her position in the form of several concise propositions. Then one deduces from these propositions yet other propositions — which may not be obvious at first glance but which the opponent must agree to since they follow in a strictly logical fashion — that contradict something in the original set of propositions. The attempt is to show that something must be askew in the original propositions since they contain a hidden contradiction.

We can outline Socrates' argument as follows: First he has Thrasymachus state his basic position in two concise propositions:

A. *Just persons are bad (they practice vice).*
B. *Unjust persons are good (they practice virtue).*

Socrates then gets Thrasymachus to expand on his position by adding to *A* and *B* some other statements. Thrasymachus agrees to do so, believing that they are innocuous enough and that they assert nothing that is incompatible with *A* and *B*:

C. *Just persons try to outdo only those who are unlike themselves.* That is, just persons try to outdo only the unjust.

D. *Unjust persons try to outdo both those who are unlike themselves and those who are like themselves.* That is, unjust persons try to outdo both the just and the unjust.

The idea behind *C* and *D* seems to be that just persons would not try to get more than other just persons. If what just persons have is justly deserved, other just persons would not want more than that, in the sense that they would not want more that what is justly deserved. On the other hand, unjust persons have things that are not justly deserved, and, having no compunctions about just deserts at all, would want more than what other persons have unjustly as well as more than what other persons have justly.

E. *Persons who are really* like *another person* are *what that person is in regard to the characteristic in question.* For example, if I am really *like* a musician, then I must *be* a musician.

F. *Knowledgeable (or wise) persons try to outdo only those unlike themselves.* That is, those who are knowledgeable try to outdo only the ignorant.

G. *Ignorant persons try to outdo both those unlike themselves and those who are like themselves.* That is, ignorant persons try to outdo both the knowledgeable and the ignorant. The idea behind *F* and *G* seems to be that if knowledge is knowledge (if truth is truth), then wise persons would not consider themselves superior to other wise persons. For example, persons who really know how to tune a lyre would not try to outdo other persons who really know how to tune one, since all would be applying the same knowledge. They would, however, try to outdo persons who do not know how to tune a lyre. By contrast, really ignorant persons, being so ignorant that they do not know they are ignorant, consider themselves superior both to other ignorant persons and to persons who are actually wise. Not knowing that they do not know how to really tune a lyre, they would try to outdo not only attempts by other ignorant persons but also attempts by those with real knowledge.

H. *Knowledgeable persons are good persons; ignorant persons are bad persons.*

After making sure that Thrasymachus agrees to all of the above statements, Socrates draws a few simple logical inferences from them, producing two additional propositions:

I. *Just persons are like knowledgeable and good persons, in that both just persons and knowledgeable and good persons try to outdo only those who are unlike themselves.*

J. *Unjust persons are like ignorant and bad persons, in that both unjust persons and ignorant and bad persons try to outdo both those who are unlike themselves and those who are like themselves.*

By this time, Thrasymachus smells a rat, but he cannot deny *I* or *J*. Proposition *I* follows logically from *C*, *F*, and *H*, to which he has already agreed; and *J* follows logically from *D*, *G*, and *H*, to which he has already agreed.

All that remains is for Socrates to draw two final inferences:

K. *Therefore just persons are knowledgeable and good (they practice virtue).*

L. *Therefore unjust persons are ignorant and bad (they practice vice).*

Thrasymachus cannot deny *K* or *L*. *K* follows logically from *E* and *I*, to which he has already agreed; and *L* follows logically from *E* and *J*, to which he has already agreed. The problem is that *K* is a direct contradiction of *A*, and that *L* is a direct contradiction of *B*. Since *A* and *K* cannot both be true, and since *B* and *L* cannot both be true, there is something terribly wrong with Thrasymachus's beginning propositions.

You might protest that the whole argument is rather contrived and that Thrasymachus is stupid for agreeing to propositions *C* through *H* if he expects to hold on to *A* and *B*; he should have seen the blind alley he was being led into. I confess that parts of the argument strike me, too, as contrived. The idea of "outdoing" is especially problematic. It is not clear that it retains exactly the same meaning in the various contexts in which Socrates uses it, but he overlooks these possible differences in his generalizations that just persons are like knowledgeable persons (since they both try to outdo only those who are unlike themselves) and that unjust persons are like ignorant persons (since both try to outdo both those who are unlike themselves and those who are like themselves).

But remember that even Socrates admits that none of the arguments in Book I establish anything about justice itself. You should note, in fact, that *reductio ad absurdum* arguments never establish a true view; they can only bring to light hidden contradictions in false views. I am suggesting that Plato was not out to convince persons like Thrasymachus of anything positive about justice; rather, his effort was aimed at demonstrating that the equation of justice and legality, and the disavowal of normative discourse implied by this equation, inevitably results in contorted views that cannot be sustained.

Interpreted in this way, the contrived character of Socrates argument is perhaps a fitting response to Thrasymachus's assertion that injustice is virtue. There is something a little too self-consciously triumphal about Thrasymachus's declaration. It is easy to imagine him glancing about the room to catch the others' reactions to such a seemingly radical statement. One wonders if he is trying to use shock effect as a substitute for good argument. This may be why Socrates asks Thrasymachus if he really means what he says, as if he suspects him of being insincere in his pronouncements. When Thrasymachus insists that he is serious, Socrates proceeds to fight contrivance with contrivance. If Plato is dramatizing the point that inquiry into a sense of justice that goes beyond mere legality is a worthy and, in fact, unavoidable enterprise, maybe the contrived character of some of the details of the argument is excusable.

Socrates' argument regarding justice among the members of a city, an army, or even a band of robbers has a similar thrust (351c–352b). The members of a band of robbers, for instance, might be viewed as

living proof of Thrasymachus's claim that injustice is good. In break-
ing the law, robbers are unjust, and they are living profitably in being
unjust. Socrates argues, however, that unless the members of the
band govern the interactions among themselves according to some
conception of justice that goes beyond legality they could not even
be profitable robbers. For example, if they are to avoid falling into
quarrelsome factions, they would presumably have to adhere to
some standard for justly distributing the loot among themselves. And
they could hardly define this standard of just distribution by appealing to what is legal or illegal according to law. The implication is that
if even robbers cannot escape treating justice as more than a question of mere legality or illegality, then surely the rest of us cannot
escape doing so either.

ABSOLUTE PHILOSOPHY VERSUS
RELATIVE CONVENTION

Underlying the challenge to Thrasymachus's equation of justice and
legality is a concern that I have not yet made explicit. Thrasymachus
insists that the formal standard of justice — obedience to laws
skewed to the advantage of those who make them—"is the same
everywhere" (339a). Since the sort of persons who are the strongest
may vary from society to society, however, thus resulting in different
laws, the particulars of what is just and unjust will vary from society
to society according to Thrasymachus's definition. To put it in modern terms, justice is culturally relative; there is no unvarying content
to the standard of justice, no content that holds good across societies
in all places and at all times.

Many scholars argue that this relativism is a special target of
Plato's *Republic*. Ancient Greece (Plato was born in 428 B.C.) was
not a unified country or nation-state as it is today. It consisted of separate city-states, such as Athens, Sparta, and Thebes, each with its
own form of government. Although these city-states often entered
into alliances when wars broke out either among themselves or with
non-Greek states such as Macedon, Persia, and Carthage, each was

sovereign over its own territory (which included the city and the surrounding countryside). As interaction in the form of trade and war alliances among the city-states increased, and people became more knowledgeable about how societies other than their own were governed, the question arose as to what form of government is best. Many Greeks tended to assume that the society in which they lived was the best because it was established by the gods. Persons like Thrasymachus, though, were suggesting that there is no best form, that there are only variations, one form being no better than another.

Such a view can have a destabilizing effect. While many persons believe the society in which they live is the best, there will always be others who are unhappy with the way they are being governed. If there is nothing sacred or special about any particular form of government, if no form is inherently superior, then critics can argue that there is no good reason for prohibiting change. If the form of government under which one is living is not the work of the gods, but merely an accident of cultural circumstances—if it developed as a matter of habit, custom, and convention, some of which is formalized into law (the Greek word *nomos* refers to all of these)—then persons who hold this relative view might feel legitimate in altering things to suit their preferences.

Plato longed for stability. In his lifetime Athens had gone from a democracy to the tyranny of a few and back to democracy. Yet he could not oppose change per se since, as we shall see, he despised democracy. He wanted Athens to change from democracy to what he thought would be a more just form of government; but if justice is equated with legality, then it makes no sense to assume that a given set of laws (or the government that makes them) is more just than another set of laws. To define justice as whatever is legal within a given society makes it impossible to ask what system of laws is the most just—something Plato clearly wanted to do. Thus, we can interpret the thrust of Socrates' arguments against Thrasymachus as an attempt to open up a discussion of the best form of government and the most just society.

We can now draw together the threads of my interpretation of Book I thus far. Life includes both action and spontaneous reflection on action. Philosophy is a developed reflective response to problems rooted in ordinary life. Life is complicated; things are not always what they appear to be. We often make statements in casual conversation that we presume to be true without knowing why they are true. Our views are frequently inherited; we take them over uncritically from our parents or other figures commonly recognized as authorities. The sociology of knowledge suggests that the truth of such views may be suspect. So-called common sense cannot serve as an unquestionable foundation for the truth since common sense is only a distillation of inherited, habitual, and customary ways of thinking, which may be wrong. Plato does not want to remain in doubt about the truth of our beliefs, especially those that pertain to such matters as justice. Socrates remarks that justice is a serious matter and concerns no less than how we ought to live (344d–e, 352d). Talk about justice is inherently normative, and we cannot avoid it even if we try. Plato conceives of philosophy as including normative discourse and as a way of answering normative questions without resorting to relativism; he sees it as a means for providing answers that will be true for societies at all times and places.

THE NORMATIVE/EMPIRICAL DISTINCTION IN A MORALIZED COSMOS

Plato does not spell out his own philosophy in Book I. As I have suggested, Book I is more an attempt to show the necessity of philosophy by dramatizing the problems to which it responds. Even at this early stage, however, we can get some grasp of the broad outlines of Plato's philosophy. I introduced the modern distinction between empirical and normative inquiry to help you understand Socrates' response to Thrasymachus. We now return to a fuller discussion of this distinction so you can see just how radically different Plato's total vision is from that of many modern philosophers.

Plato clearly supports the idea that there is a kind of inquiry that investigates not how people do actually behave but how they ought to behave, the sort of inquiry that I called normative. When I introduced the difference between empirical and normative inquiry, however, I remarked that today it is often used synonymously with the fact/value distinction. Plato would have been baffled by this latter distinction, since for him — if we stick to using these terms — *values are themselves facts*. Values are as objective for Plato as scientific facts, such as the fact that a molecule of water contains two atoms of hydrogen and one atom of oxygen, are for us. The problem is that the empirical/normative distinction is itself loaded with assumptions that would have puzzled Plato.

We moderns think of the sciences as empirical enterprises, which describe and explain facts, whereas normative inquiry addresses the issue of values. The term *empirical* is now used to describe knowledge based on experience, and, more specifically, knowledge based on what we can observe through at least one of the five senses. Plato would agree that normative inquiry produces knowledge that is not derived through the senses; as you will see later, he believes that the senses are very deceiving and cannot produce sure, or certain, knowledge. But Plato also believes that even sure knowledge of nature cannot not be based on the senses. He does not divide the cosmos into a world of facts, which we can know through the senses disciplined by the methods of the sciences, and a world of values, which we can know through normative inquiry. Rather, the whole cosmos is a moral one through and through; *nature* (the Greek word is *physis*) includes not only facts such as those regarding water, but also facts about values, and sure knowledge of nature comes only through philosophy.

Plato's hope for philosophy was that it could answer normative questions, or questions about how we ought to live, by discerning what nature really is. His project, to frame it in terms that he would have used, is to replace *nomos* with knowledge of *physis*, or at least to transform *nomos* by basing it on *physis*. Recall that *nomos* refers to what is right and proper by custom and convention. It includes traditional ways of behaving that are habitual and unconscious as well as standards that are codified into formal laws. *Nomos* refers to those standards of behavior that might vary from culture to culture. Knowledge of *physis* is knowledge of how we ought to live if we live according to *nature*, which is universal and invariant, the same for all times and places.

Physis, or nature, as you might have guessed, is the word from which our term *physics* derives. But whereas we conceive of physics as a study of facts, as distinguished from values, Plato does not narrow nature down to a world that does not include values. As different as Plato's use of *nature* is from our use of the term, though, there are some important similarities. When we say something is natural, we mean to say that it is given or just there; it is objective and not something that could be otherwise. Something that is natural is not the product of human creation in general and certainly not the result of individual subjective choices and preferences. Plato's use of *physis* includes these same connotations. Philosophy, as knowledge of how we ought to behave according to nature, discovers standards that are given, truly objective, and not the result of human creation or individual choices.

Plato's vision of a moralized cosmos is very difficult for us to grasp, in part because, whether we know it or not, we have all been influenced to some extent by modern philosophers. But you must try to work your way into a sympathetic appreciation of it if you are to understand the rest of the *Republic*. It is worth the effort since it will make you more fully aware of the implications of your own view of things. A good way to understand more fully what you believe is to compare it to something radically different. A look at the last argument in Book I will begin to acclimate you to the broader vision of the world within which Plato operates.

The argument reconsiders Thrasymachus's claim that the unjust live happier and better lives (352d–354a). Socrates begins by getting Thrasymachus to agree that everything has a function (the Greek is *ergon)*, something that it does uniquely or at least better than anything else. We can do things with horses that it would be hard to do with anything else. We can say the same thing about eyes, ears, and pruning knives. Socrates then gets Thrasymachus to agree that corresponding to the function of a thing is a virtue (the Greek is *aretē*, sometimes translated as "excellence"), that which allows the thing to perform its function well. After Thrasymachus also agrees that the

function of the soul (Greek *psychē*, sometimes translated as "mind")
is to deliberate, rule over the whole person, and generally take care
of matters important to life, Socrates goes for the kill. Since corresponding to each thing's function is a virtue that allows a thing to
perform its function well, the soul, too, has a virtue; and since Thrasymachus has supposedly already agreed in a previous argument that
justice is a soul's virtue, Socrates concludes that it is justice that
allows a person to deliberate and rule over one's life well. Finally,
since deliberating and ruling over one's life well are necessary to
happiness, a just person will be happier than an unjust person.

Socrates' argument is peculiar in that he seems to succeed in estab-
lishing that justice is the virtue that will allow a person to live a happier life even though he has yet to provide a positive conception of
what justice itself is. Earlier, though, Socrates pointed out this failing
in all the arguments in Book I. Equally peculiar, to modern readers, is
Socrates' use of the term *virtue*. When we say a person is virtuous, we
mean that the person is moral, and to talk about the virtue of a horse,
our eyes, or pruning knives is to stretch the meaning of the word so far
that it seems to lose all meaning. But we must look more closely at the
connotations that the term *virtue* has for us, for they take on a very different meaning when embedded in Plato's vision of a moralized cosmos.

Plato's use of *virtue* to refer to that which allows a thing to perform
its function well would not have been controversial at the time, and it
may not be as peculiar even for us as it first seems. Consider the meaning of *virtue* in the sentence "The virtue of driving to the mall rather
than walking is that you are not as tired when you get there." It is not
hard to imagine someone making this statement and being understood,
even though the sentence clearly does not mean that persons who
walk to the mall are immoral, whereas those who drive are moral.
Indeed, we seem to be very close here to Plato's sense of the term, and
the connection is clearer, perhaps, when *aretē* is translated as "excellence." The virtue of driving is that it gets us to the mall most efficiently,
with much less expenditure of energy than if we walked. Similarly, if I
say, "The virtue of carrying water in a bucket rather than in our hands
is that we spill less," my statement is quite intelligible; it means that
buckets are much better designed for carrying water than are hands, or
that buckets, by their very nature, function better to carry water.

Now, this sense of virtue, which we take to be completely separate from moral considerations, connects with the moral sense of the term in Plato's broader vision. In Plato's view, we discover the standard for virtue, or how we ought to live, by finding out what we really are by nature, by discovering the function assigned to us by the scheme of the cosmos. And that function is as natural, given, objective, and independent of human choice and preference as are the functions assigned by nature to eyes, ears, horses, pruning knives, and buckets. (Pruning knives and buckets, of course, are human artifacts; we make them. But if pruning knives are actually to cut vines and buckets are actually to carry water, we are going to have to attend, in making them, to facts and principles that are not of our making.)

We find Plato's use of the term *virtue* in Socrates' last argument against Thrasymachus, where he moves easily from talking about the virtue of pruning knives to the virtue of the soul, to be peculiar because we tend to place the facts of nature — what it is that enables eyes, ears, horses, pruning knives, and buckets to do what they do best — in a category completely separate from the moral question of how we ought to live. The facts of nature are objective, we believe, and we can know them with a fair degree of certainty. Answers to the question of how we ought to live our lives are another matter. In this area, there is no certainty; even if the answers are not simply the product of individual subjective preferences, the best that we can say is that they vary from culture to culture. For Plato, it is this separation that would be peculiar; for him, to discover how we ought to live our lives is to discover a universal natural fact about ourselves.

The most general way of expressing the unbridgeable gulf that many moderns see between the empirical and the normative, between facts and values, is to say that what ought to be cannot be derived from what is. Facts are what is (they are given by nature and are determined by one kind of inquiry), and values are what ought to be (they are not given by nature and are determined by a wholly different kind of inquiry), and never the twain shall meet. Plato's general philosophical position is summarized in the rejection of this formula. In his cosmos, we discover what ought to be precisely by discovering what really, by nature, we are.

I do not mean to suggest that all modern philosophers and theorists accept the empirical/normative and fact/value distinctions. Many persons challenge their tenability, frequently arguing that we need to reestablish connections with older ways of thinking, especially Greek ways of thinking. But the fact that such arguments are made is evidence that most modern thinkers, rightly or wrongly, have abandoned Plato's vision of a moralized cosmos.

Some Greek philosophers other than Plato were also disturbed about basing standards for how we ought to live on individual subjective choices at worst and culturally relative *nomos* at best; they too sought the authority of *physis*. For many of them, however, the authority of nature is ultimately rooted in divine authority. For Plato, philosophy must ascend to knowledge of nature without the help of any external authorities, including religious ones. Socrates says that we can sort out the true and the false in what Thrasymachus asserts by the following method:

> If we oppose him with a parallel speech about the blessings of the just life, and then he replies, and then we do, we'd have to count and measure the good things mentioned on each side, and we'd need a jury to decide the case. But if, on the other hand, we investigate the question, as we've been doing, by seeking agreement with each other, we ourselves can be both jury and advocates at once. (348a–b)

Philosophy, in other words, must be its own jury. It begins in ordinary life, in which *nomos* rules the day more often than not, but if it is to get beyond subjective choices and mere custom and convention and rise to a knowledge of *physis*, it cannot lapse back into appeals to customarily recognized external authorities, even if those authorities are religious ones. Philosophy pulls itself out of *nomos* and up to objective knowledge of *physis* by its own bootstraps.

PLATO'S DIALOGICAL STYLE RECONSIDERED

The claim that philosophy proceeds by pitting speech against speech, by what Plato will later call dialectic, brings us to a fuller discussion of Plato's dramatic or dialogical style. Recognizing that the term *dialectic* and our words *dialect* and *dialogue* all refer to speech and speaking, we might argue that Plato writes in the dialogical form in an attempt to mimic the method by which he believes philosophy advances.

This suggestion, however, is subject to the objection I noted at the beginning of the chapter, that the dialogue of the *Republic* has a contrived feeling about it. While Socrates' interlocutors are not completely implausible fabrications, it is impossible to characterize much of the *Republic* as a genuine debate in which speech is pitted against speech. In stretches of the text that go on for pages, the other participants' contributions consist only of "Yes," "Certainly," "That's right," "We should agree to that," and so forth. If philosophy advances toward the truth through dialogue and debate, and if Plato is trying to imitate in his style the method of philosophy, then why is so much of his so-called dialogue a barely disguised monologue?

I do not know of any attempts to answer this question that are wholly satisfactory, but most scholars begin by noting the fact that many of the characters who appear in the *Republic* were also actual, historical persons. The most important is Socrates, who was Plato's teacher. Since the historical Socrates did not write anything of his own, all that we know about him and his views must be gleaned from Plato's dialogues and the texts of a few other Greek writers: Xenophon, Aristophanes, and Aristotle. Although the various representations of Socrates are not always consistent, they all point to a person who made it his life's mission to wander about Athens challenging his fellow citizens' beliefs. He apparently saw himself as a full-time gadfly, intent on spurring others to dedicate their lives to the search for truth and virtue by getting them to see the inconsistencies and incoherences in their easygoing, conventional views (see the *Apology*, another of Plato's dialogues, 30e–31a). Plato himself had apparently engaged in many conversations with Socrates and felt in debt to him for much that he had learned. Another explanation for Plato's choice of the dialogical style, then, is that he wanted to honor his teacher by preserving in his own writing something of the way Socrates went about the business of philosophizing through oral discourse. On this account, the mystery of Plato's style is further deflated by the fact that it was hardly unique; other associates of Socrates also composed dialogues in which Socrates appeared as a character.

But this explanation for Plato's dialogical style is too simple. If we assume that Plato was heavily influenced by the historical Socrates, should we take everything that the Socrates of Plato's dialogues says to represent the views of the historical Socrates? How much of what the character Socrates says is the view of the historical Socrates, and how much of it might be Plato's view put into the mouth of the character Socrates? One answer, no longer very common among scholars, is that everything Plato has Socrates say should be taken to represent the historical Socrates. A more frequent reply today is that the Socrates in Plato's early dialogues (Plato was quite prolific, and the corpus, or body, of his work is vast) closely reflects the views of the historical Socrates. As Plato emerged from the influence of his teacher and developed into a thinker in his own right, the character of Socrates comes to serve more as a mouthpiece for Plato's own views. By this interpretation, the dramatic form becomes less central to Plato's purpose in his later writings. In one of his last works, *The Laws*, the character of Socrates is missing altogether, and some scholars even speculate that it was first written in normal essay form and then rather mechanically put into dialogical form.

The *Republic* is usually dated as a middle work, but many commentators see a shift in style within the *Republic* itself. Book I, according to this view, is continuous with the style of Plato's earlier dialogues, in which characters other than Socrates make arguments of their own, albeit ones that are finally upset by Socrates. It is after Book I that the other characters are reduced to passive yea-sayers and Socrates becomes more of a teacher, if not a preacher, than an interlocutor on a par with the other characters. Some scholars argue that the shift is so dramatic that Plato must have composed Book I earlier, as an independent dialogue, and then returned to make use of it as an introduction to the *Republic*.

Other scholars see something more complicated going on in the shift within the *Republic*. They contend that Plato's shift after Book I represents a criticism of the historical Socrates, although Plato still honors his teacher by retaining him as the central character in the work. Although the historical Socrates thought one should live one's life in pursuit of truth and virtue, he never claimed to actually know any final truths. His wisdom, he claimed, was in his recognition of his ignorance. When he declared that "the unexamined life is not worth living" (*Apology*, 38a), he seems to have meant that worthiness lies in the search for the truth rather than in its discovery. According to these scholars, the Socrates of Book I, who unsettles the conventional views of the other conversationalists but does not seem particularly disturbed to confess at the end that he has no positive doctrines of his own, represents the historical Socrates. The Socrates after Book I, in contrast, articulates Plato's own view that the discovery of ultimate truths is possible.

In a similar vein, the shift in style within the *Republic* may reflect Plato's criticism of Socrates' method of philosophizing and an assumption on which that method rests. While Book I seems to clear the ground for a presentation of Plato's own views, as I have suggested, it may also be meant to portray the futility of Socrates' approach to philosophy. The historical Socrates seems to have been democratic in outlook, believing that all persons could be drawn into conversation that would set them in pursuit of truth and a virtuous life. The opening scene of the *Republic* seems to cast doubt on Socrates' democratic assumption. When Polemarchus and his friends run into Socrates and Glaucon, who are on their way back to Athens from the religious festival, Polemarchus asserts, "Well, you must either prove stronger than we are, or you will have to stay here." When Socrates asks if persuasion rather than force would do, Polemarchus asks in return, "But could you persuade us, if we won't listen?" (327c) It is Glaucon who may provide Plato's own answer: "Certainly not."

The early and abrupt departure of Cephalus, the father of Polemarchus, may also be intended to dramatize Plato's belief that some people are so entrenched in conventional views that they are beyond the reach of philosophical conversation. And while Thrasymachus stays for the discussion and says at the appropriate times that he agrees with Socrates, he clearly is not persuaded. He admits on several occasions that the only reason he says he agrees is to please Socrates and to avoid being unpopular with the rest of those present (350e, 351c, 350e). He, too, seems to be beyond the reach of philosophy.

Plato apparently believes that even among those who can be genuinely engaged in philosophy, not all will be capable of pursuing it far enough. He seems to think that while philosophy starts out by pitting speech against speech, it cannot stop there, as it does for the historical Socrates, if it is actually to discover final truths. The style of Books II–X of the *Republic*, then, in which Socrates holds forth with little meaningful participation by the other interlocutors, dramatizes, by its contrast with the style of Book I, Plato's contention that the conversational style of philosophizing practiced by the historical Socrates is limited in what it can accomplish. If Plato sees himself not as working out his philosophy in a genuine conversation but as reporting the truths he has already discovered to those who are at least capable of listening, then the pontificating manner he gives to Socrates after Book I is quite apt. (For those incapable even of listening to a report of the truth, Plato, as we will see, has other means to get them to live a virtuous life.)

This extended account of the relationship between Plato and the historical Socrates, and of how that relationship is reflected in the shift in style within the *Republic*, can accommodate most of what I have to say in the following chapters. Given Socrates' profound influence on Plato, however, Plato's critical struggle against Socrates may reflect a struggle occurring within Plato himself. To try to sort out precisely what in the *Republic* should be attributed to the historical Socrates and what to Plato may be to draw lines that are clearer than any Plato himself could have drawn. In any case, since subsequent chapters will be dealing with Books II–X of the *Republic*, I will hereafter treat the views spoken by Socrates as Plato's own unless I indicate otherwise.

SOME INITIAL RESERVATIONS

Before proceeding to the next chapter, I should admit my own reservations about Plato's conception of, and hope for, philosophy. I agree that philosophy is rooted in ordinary life. The concern with the distinction between appearance and reality, which is at the heart of philosophy, arises from the common experience of discovering that we no longer believe what we once believed, that things are not always what they seem. I share with Plato a distrust of what customarily recognized authorities claim to be true. It seems to me, too, that the appeal to so-called common sense to settle disputes about what is real often serves to short-circuit debate rather than settle it. The appeal to common sense too frequently functions as another way of saying "I'm right, you're wrong, and that's that." I also agree that normative discourse is inescapable. To live is to make choices, and it seems dishonest to claim that those choices are not based on what one believes ought to be.

I have reservations, however, as to whether philosophy can actually fulfill Plato's hopes for it. Plato would have philosophy be its own jury; he sees in it the capacity to get beyond all that is merely customary and conventional, relative and subjective. For him, philosophy can tell us what is true according to the very nature of the cosmos. But philosophy does not conduct itself. It is a reflective activity practiced by human beings, and there is no surefire method for escaping the biases of culturally rooted custom, convention, and common sense. Try as we might to get out from under them, these influences will inevitably cloud our vision. Furthermore, is the cosmos really an inherently moral order with values already there, given, woven into the very scheme of nature, waiting to be discovered? Perhaps it is the distinctive predicament of human beings to have to inject values into a cosmos that is indifferent to their plight. We are saddled with serious problems if this is the case, for unless we all inject compatible values into the cosmos, conflict is inevitable. While such problems may spur the search for a solution, there is no guarantee that a solution can be found.

Also, there is supreme irony in the fact that philosophy can lead philosophers to forget its origin in ordinary life. Philosophy can easily come to be viewed as a diversion from life, and perhaps even as an escape from life. I will suggest later that Plato is seduced by this possibility. One of the reasons the *Republic* is particularly useful as an introduction to philosophy is that it shows both how philosophy can help us wrestle with the problems of ordinary life and how it can offer an escape from life.

Suggestions for Further Reading

GENERAL

Most translations of the *Republic* include introductory essays and book-by-book summaries. Cornford, for example, intersperses commentary throughout his translation. The interpretative books on the *Republic* that are most intellectually accessible to nonspecialists include *An Introduction to Plato's "Republic,"* by Julia Annas; *Plato's "Republic:" A Philosophical Commentary*, by R. C. Cross and A. D. Woozley; *Plato and the "Republic,"* by Nickolas Pappas; and *A Companion to "Plato's Republic,"* by Nicholas P. White. Two books, not devoted exclusively to the *Republic*, that introduce Plato's ideas to nonspecialists are George Klosko's *The Development of Plato's Political Theory* and Irving M. Zeitlin's *Plato's Vision: The Classical Origins of Social and Political Thought*.

Readers interested in pursuing further research on the *Republic* or Plato's thought generally might begin with the above works. In later chapters, I will refer to them where they provide particularly interesting interpretations or ones that contrast with my own. Some of the above authors arrange material thematically; others more or less follow Plato's own order of exposition. Most of them include copious references to even more specialized works, both books and journal articles, on the many aspects of Plato's thought.

A convenient way to sample some of the more specialized secondary literature directly is to look at books that are collections of essays by different authors. Recommended in this vein is *Plato: A Collection of Critical Essays*, edited by Gregory Vlastos (vol. 1, *Metaphysics and Epistemology*; vol. 2, *Ethics, Politics, and Philosophy of Art and Religion*). Again, you can find hundreds of references to additional secondary literature in these works. *New Essays on Plato and Aristotle*, edited by Renford Bambrough, is a similar volume.

SUGGESTIONS RELATING TO PARTICULAR
POINTS IN CHAPTER 1

More than anyone else, Karl Marx is responsible for making the sociology of knowledge commonplace in modern social thought. The basic notion behind the sociology of knowledge is easily seen in his famous statement in part 1 of the *Manifesto of the Communist Party* that the "ruling ideas of each age have ever been the ideas of its ruling class." He gives a more extended explanation of this claim in part 1 of *The German Ideology*.

The most famous work of Alfred North Whitehead, the twentieth-century philosopher who said that western philosophy is a "series of footnotes" to Plato, and who argues that philosophy is a critic of common sense, is *Process and Reality*. See part 1, Chapter 1, for his remarks on the general nature of philosophy; the quip about Plato is in part 2, chapter 1. *Process and Reality* is a notoriously difficult work, however, even for those who have already studied philosophy intensively. Readers interested in Whitehead, who is notable because he draws so self-consciously upon some of Plato's most important doctrines, will find his *Adventures of Ideas* and *Modes of Thought* much easier to understand.

Klosko's *The Development of Plato's Political Theory* has a good discussion on pages 2–5 of the distinction between *physis* and *nomos*, and Plato's attack on conventionalism and relativism. Grube also sees conventionalism and relativism as primary targets of the *Republic*. He touches briefly on the topic in the introduction to his translation of the *Republic* (p. xi) and at greater length in chapter 1 of his *Plato's Thought*.

The is/ought and fact/value distinctions upheld by many modern thinkers are usually traced to the eighteenth-century Scottish philosopher David Hume, whose most important work is *A Treatise of Human Nature*. See especially book 3, part 1. The variety of efforts to loosen these distinctions by recurring to Greek thought is illustrated in the works of Whitehead and Alasdair MacIntyre. See chapters 6–8 of Whitehead's *Modes of Thought* and MacIntyre's *After Virtue*.

For a further discussion of the various views of Plato's relationship to the historical Socrates, and its bearing on how the remarks of the Socrates who appears in the *Republic* should be interpreted, see Klosko's *The Development of Plato's Political Theory*, chapters 1 and 2. See also Annas's *An Introduction to Plato's "Republic,"* chapters 1 and 2. C. D. C.

Reeve's *Philosopher-Kings*, chapter 1, offers an even more nuanced account, but one that nonspecialists will find considerably more difficult to follow. Plato's *Apology*, in which Socrates says that the "unexamined life is not worth living" and in which he is described as a "gadfly," is included in the collection of Jowett's translations of Plato's dialogues. It is also in Rouse's collection. Aristophanes gives an account of Socrates in his drama *The Clouds*. Xenophon's account of Socrates is found in his *Memorabilia*.

2

Politics and the Ideal City: Books II–V

—〰—

PLATO VERSUS HOBBES ON JUSTICE AND HAPPINESS

It becomes obvious in the opening of Book II that Thrasymachus is not alone in his view of justice. Socrates has convinced Glaucon and Adeimantus that something is wrong with Thrasymachus's position, but they are not confident that he has undermined it completely. They seem to believe that Thrasymachus is simply a poor defender of a very widespread view that may after all have considerable merit to it.

To provide a better description of what he believes is the most common view of justice, Glaucon introduces a taxonomy, or system of classification, for things that are good (357a–358a). Some things, he says, are good in themselves; their goodness stands on its own and requires nothing else to justify it. Other things are good only in a secondary sense; they are not good in themselves, but they are instrumental in producing other things that are good in themselves. A middle category comprises things that are good in themselves and that produce other good things as well.

Glaucon reports that what he hears from most people is that justice is good but only in the secondary, instrumental sense. If one could be certain of always being on the giving end of injustice, the practice of justice would be foolish. People recognize, however, that they are going to be on the receiving end of injustice as often as not, and that suffering injustice is naturally bad. Thus, they strike a compromise: they enter into a compact or contract with each other, promising not to do injustice to others if others, in return, will not do injustice to them, and proceed to set up a system of laws prescribing what people can and cannot do. Justice turns out to be, as Thrasymachus said, obedience to the laws, and people practice justice, not because they believe it is good in itself, but because they know they are not powerful enough to always be on the giving rather than the receiving end of injustice.

Consider the story, Glaucon says, of the shepherd who discovers a magical ring that allows him to become invisible when he chooses (359b–360d). Here is a person who could always dish out injustice without ever suffering it. That most people find his behavior entirely plausible—his killing of the king, theft of the king's wife, and takeover of the kingdom—confirms that they do not consider justice to be good in itself. Most people know they would do exactly the same thing as the shepherd does if they could get away with it. Were we to update this ancient tale, we might say that the most amazing thing about Superman is not that he can jump tall buildings in a single bound but that he always uses that power for good purposes.

Glaucon finds this view of justice unappealing and insists repeatedly that it is not his own, that all he is doing is reporting what others say. It is tempting to view Glaucon as rather cowardly, in that he seems to hide behind what others say; Thrasymachus at least claims his view as his own. The point of Plato's depiction of Glaucon, however, is that even though he says he rejects the prevalent view of justice, he is in no better position than Thrasymachus unless he knows why he rejects it. Glaucon admits that he does not know why the view he rejects is wrong. He wants to believe that justice is something nobler and grander, that it is a good in itself, and that a person who practices justice for its own sake would be the truly happiest person, but he has no grounds for holding this view. So, he asks Socrates to demonstrate the truth of what he wants to believe.

✳Glaucon and Socrates agree that justice is in the middle category of things that are good — it is both a good in itself and a good that produces other goods. But the problem is this: How are we to be sure justice produces happiness because it is ultimately good in itself rather than because of the secondary benefits it also produces? The reputation for being just and the goods and honors one enjoys because of that reputation are secondary benefits of justice and are not to be disparaged. Persons with a reputation for being just, Glaucon says, will be entrusted with responsibility for ruling, will get the best business contracts, and will usually be able to marry the spouse of their choice (362a–c). This would be especially true in a society that generally lives by the contract Glaucon had already described. These benefits are not bad, but they are not the real reasons why one should practice justice; they are only incidental benefits. Unless some means is devised to separate clearly the happiness produced by the incidental benefits of justice from the happiness that results from the practice of justice for its own sake, there will always be room for suspicion that the happiness Socrates ascribes to justice itself actually derives entirely from its secondary benefits.

Glaucon therefore devises an extraordinarily stringent test for Socrates (360e–361d): He asks him to demonstrate that a person who is really just but who has a false reputation for being unjust will truly be more happy than a person who is really unjust but through deceit has a false reputation for being just. If Socrates succeeds under these conditions, we can be sure that the person who is really just is happier only because of the practice of justice for its own sake, and not because of its secondary benefits, since the just person's false reputation for being unjust will deny him or her all the secondary benefits.

Adeimantus adds a further element to the test by extending its conditions into the afterlife (362d–367e). Even if Socrates can show that the just person will be happier than the unjust person in this life, if their false reputations do not continue into the afterlife, we still cannot be sure that the happiness of the just person derives only from the practice of justice for its own sake. If the gods see through the false reputations and finally reward the truly just person and punish the truly unjust person, how do we know that the just person was not practicing justice all along for the payoff in the afterlife? Thus, Adeimantus says, Socrates must prove that just persons would practice justice and be happier even if a mistaken reputation for injustice before the gods denied them the secondary benefits bestowed in the afterlife. Prove that, Adeimantus says, and Socrates has really proven something.

Before looking at how Socrates proposes to go about his demonstration, we should pause to consider a little more closely the nature of the debate at hand by putting it in the context of the issues we discussed in chapter 1. The question is how the practice of justice for its own sake is related to happiness. Is there a real happiness, a true and higher sort of happiness, that can be distinguished from a happiness that is only apparent and lesser but that we too often take to be the only sort of happiness? And is this real happiness produced by conforming ourselves to a standard of justice that is independent of human contrivance, compacts, and agreements, one that is woven into the very fabric of the cosmos? Or is justice purely the invention of human beings? Is it merely obedience to rules of behavior we agree upon in order to survive and enjoy what we ordinarily take to be happiness?

Glaucon's description of the widespread view of justice is particularly interesting because it is strikingly similar to the view of Thomas Hobbes, an English philosopher of the seventeenth century who has had a big influence on subsequent modern thought. According to Hobbes, we are all egoists always looking out for number one. Happiness is a matter of fulfilling our desires and acquiring the power to do so. Since our desires differ, and since we can never be sure of having enough power to fulfill them, serious conflict is inevitable. Existence becomes "a perpetual and restless desire of power after power, that ceaseth only in death." Life would be "solitary, poor, nasty, brutish, and short," Hobbes writes in another famous line, were it not for a compromise struck by individuals. We recognize that if we seek to fulfill all our desires by whatever means possible, most of us are not going to be very happy; we are going to end up dead and unable to fulfill any of our desires. So, we enter into a social contract with each other. We come to some agreement as to what kinds of behavior are allowed, or agree to appoint a special person or group of persons to make that determination, and agree to abide by it. Justice is obedience to the agreement and injustice disobedience. There is nothing grand or noble about justice in any cosmic sense; it is simply the product of a little practical wisdom on the part of creatures who want to enjoy the happiness of surviving and the fulfillment of at least some of their very mundane desires. The difference between the view of justice Socrates is asked to defend and the view reported by Glaucon and Adeimantus to be common in ancient Greece, then, turns out to be the difference between Plato's view and one that still has many modern adherents. The differing consequences of the two views is still quite relevant today.

THE CONSTRUCTION AND RATIONALE OF THE IDEAL CITY

Socrates suggests that the best way to discover real justice is to look for it first where it is easiest to see (368c–369b). One could look for justice in a single person or in a city, he says, but the larger scale of the city might produce results more readily. After convincing the others of this strategy, Socrates sets off to construct a city in which real justice reigns. And most students sigh in relief that, finally, they are going to get to the real meat of the *Republic*.

Since the rest of the work is long, and its overall organization is easy to loose sight of amidst its many twists and turns, we should do a quick survey of Plato's general plan before proceeding with the discussion. A description of the details of the just city — the best city, the one designed according to nature — occupies the rest of Book II, Book III, and the first part of Book IV. In the remainder of Book IV, Socrates homes in on exactly what justice is in such a city and then argues that it is essentially the same thing in a single human being, the soul being parallel in structure to the city. Socrates is about to compare the happiness of the really just person with that of the really unjust person when he is challenged again on some aspects of the just city. To meet this challenge, Books V–VII backtrack to discuss in further detail matters regarding the just city that were glossed over in the first description. It is not until Books VIII–X that Socrates finally returns to the question of the happiness of the just and unjust persons.

My discussion so far has stuck pretty close to Plato's own order of exposition, but I am now going to switch gears. If I continued to take Plato's arguments one by one and devote an entire chapter to each book of the *Republic*, we could easily become lost in the details and loose track of the work's general direction. In the remaining books the order of Plato's exposition is not always the best order to follow in explaining the logic of that exposition. Thus, from here on I will move a little more quickly and draw on passages that shed light on a general point, even if doing so means taking them out of the order in which Plato presents them.

Socrates begins his description of the really just city with the claim that individual human beings are not self-sufficient. Since most of us are not self-sufficient even in providing ourselves with the requisites of physical survival, Socrates begins by designing a city to produce them (369a–372b). The city incorporates a division of labor for the provision of food, shelter, and clothing. Arguing that we are all more productive if we specialize in one thing rather than try to excel at many things, Socrates sets up the city as a community of interdependent shepherds, farmers, carpenters, weavers, cobblers, blacksmiths, traders, shopkeepers, and so forth.

Glaucon interrupts Socrates to protest that his description assumes that people want only to live, when actually they want to live well (372c–e). People want not only basic foodstuffs but relishes and other condiments, not just basic housing but fine furniture, and not just clothing but jewelry. In short, people want luxuries. Socrates agrees, but nervously, suggesting that the city he has described would be a truly healthy one and that to admit luxuries into it will

lay the groundwork for injustice. Nevertheless, he allows for luxuries
and traces the consequences (372e-374a).

First, the population increases. The persons practicing the various
crafts he has already included will have to grow in number if they are
to provide luxuries as well as necessities. Second, new tasks arise.
Doctors who can treat illnesses that result from eating exotic foods
must be brought on the scene. Third, and more important, since a
larger population entails a larger territory, there will need to be a
professional army to acquire sufficient land through war and defend
it once acquired. This whole new class of persons who specialize in
soldiering Socrates initially calls the guardians.

To the class of craftspeople and the class of guardians Socrates
adds a third: a class of overseers, or rulers, who care for the city as a
whole (412a-b). Before proceeding, I must pause to clarify a point
of nomenclature. Once Socrates has introduced the overseers, he
says he will henceforth use the term *auxiliaries* to refer to those
whom he had previously called guardians. These auxiliaries are the
helpers of the overseers. Since the overseers seem to be recruited
from the best auxiliaries, however, some of what Socrates says about
the auxiliaries also seems to apply to the overseers as well. We can
avoid confusion if we stick to the following scheme: there are two
broad classes in the city, the craftspeople and the guardians, but the
guardian class is subdivided into the class of auxiliaries and the class
of overseers, or rulers. In what follows, I will for the most part use
the terms *craftspeople*, *auxiliaries*, and *overseers* (or *rulers*); on the
few occasions that I use *guardians*, I refer to both the auxiliaries
and the overseers. (Most translations use the term *craftsmen* instead
of *craftspeople*, but since Plato includes women in this class, I will
continue to use the more inclusive term.)

When Socrates first introduces the overseers, he does not make
clear what caring for the city as a whole entails. The only function he
indicates early on is that the overseers are to educate the auxiliaries
(372e-376d). Good soldiers must be fearless and ferocious, Socrates
says, but these same characteristics should not be turned against the
population the auxiliaries are supposed to protect. Thus, the task is to
make the auxiliaries into junkyard dogs, who are ferocious toward

outsiders but gentle toward their owners. This can be done only
through proper training, and Socrates lays down the principles for
such training (376c–412b); in an actual city it would be the overseers
who put them into effect. It seems, then, that the overseers, or rulers,
are introduced only to train the auxiliaries, who, in turn, were introduced only because luxuries were admitted in the city.

This is not the whole story, though, for the rationale Plato invokes
to introduce the overseers does not begin to account for the function they play once they are on the scene. Glaucon remarks that a
city composed only of craftspeople would be no different than one
founded for pigs (372d). Organized solely for the most efficient provision of the requisites of mere physical survival, it would be a sort
of grand trough from which people obtain food, shelter, and clothing. Socrates is hesitant to allow luxuries into the picture, but Plato
would be no more satisfied with a city of craftspeople alone than is
Glaucon. Plato, too, believes that humans want not only to live but to
live well. For him, however, living well does not mean having access
to luxuries; it means living in the light of the truth. The overseers, it
turns out, must be philosophers — lovers of wisdom, learning, and
the truth — and education turns out to be not only a function of the
overseers but the primary purpose of the whole organization of the
city. The division of labor may make the production of food, shelter,
and clothing more efficient, but it does much more than that. It creates the opportunity for at least some persons to engage in philosophy, itself a specialized activity, and gain access to the truth. And the
most important part of truth goes beyond what it is necessary to
know to coordinate the activities of the craftspeople and auxiliaries
to ensure physical survival.

Underpinning Socrates' description of the best city is a complex
account of the relation between nature and nurture. On one hand,
Plato assumes that we are all born with physical and intellectual
equipment that makes us suited to perform some tasks better than
others. We are each handed certain natures that, try as we might, we
cannot alter. In fact, attempting to do what we are not fitted to do by
nature will only make us miserable. On the other hand, the equipment we are handed at birth is not sufficient to guarantee that we

will excel at the particular function nature assigns us. For that, education and training are necessary. Our natures must be nurtured if they are to bear fruit. Plato believes this to be as true of philosophy as it is of soldiering, farming, or weaving. While we all may aspire to the truth, some of us, given our natural endowments, are simply incapable of grasping it. Others are born with the natural capability of knowing the truth, but unless that capability is cultivated through a long and arduous process of education, it will come to nothing.

Plato's vision of the best city, then, boils down in its broadest outline to this: We all aspire to live in light of the truth. Recognizing, however, that we are not all equipped by nature to gain access to the truth, and that even those who do have the capacity must receive special training, we institute a division of labor. Farmers will be farmers, carpenters will be carpenters, weavers will be weavers, and soldiers will be soldiers. And philosophers, not having to worry about growing food, building houses, making clothes, or defending the city, will be afforded the opportunity to ascend through rigorous training to the apprehension of the truth. They will then govern the rest of us in the light of that truth. The organization of the city makes philosophy possible, and philosophy makes living according to the truth possible.

Plato's conception of true justice in the city works out to be a synopsis of his political vision (427d–434d). Like many of his contemporaries, Plato takes justice to be one of four cardinal virtues, the others being wisdom, courage, and moderation. Socrates says that since his best city embodies all four virtues, justice can be discovered through a process of elimination: if the other three virtues are identified first, the true nature of justice will remain as obvious. Wisdom in a wise city, he says, is lodged primarily in the class of overseers comprised of philosophers, who are, by definition, lovers of wisdom, learning, and truth. Courage, too, is located primarily within a single class, the auxiliaries, who are most in need of it. Moderation, by contrast, is spread through all the classes and is reflected in agreement about who should rule. Members of all three classes — craftspeople, auxiliaries, and philosophers alike — agree that only the philosophers should rule.

Justice, Socrates argues, is the virtue that makes all the others possible. Simply put, it is the idea that the members of the various classes should stick solely to the business for which they are suited by nature and not meddle in the functions of the other classes. There is an element of truth to the commonsense notion that justice means giving to persons what rightfully belongs to them; in what Plato regards as a deeper conception of justice, however, what "belongs" to a person must be interpreted to mean the tasks assigned to that person by nature. If the auxiliaries get interested in making shoes or ruling, they are not going to be good soldiers, and courage is undermined. If craftspeople take it into their heads to become soldiers or think they are equipped to rule, moderation is destroyed. And if philosophers occupy themselves with building houses or developing battle strategies, they are not going to be able to rise to knowledge of the truth, wisdom suffers, and the whole social structure based on that wisdom comes tumbling down.

By this time you may be chomping at the bit to ask, "But what *is* this truth under which we want to live but which we must depend on philosophers to provide?" A fair question. The only thing we have at this point is Plato's assertion that most of us cannot know the truth, and that we therefore ought to organize our societies so that those who are capable of rising to knowledge of the truth can do so. While Plato must eventually let us in on a few more elements of the truth and show how philosophers are able to apprehend it, we must suspend this demand temporarily. I will press it at greater length in the next chapter. For now, assuming that the truth is generally such as Plato claims it to be and that philosophers can know it, let us explore how the general political scheme based on these assumptions might make sense of a few of his more specific political prescriptions.

ART AND CENSORSHIP

We can begin with Plato's call for censorship. In the long section stretching from the middle of Book II (376a) to the middle of Book III (412a), he makes clear just how serious he is about the importance of nurture in the molding of individuals. The general topic of the section concerns how the auxiliaries are to be educated. (It would seem that the regimen applies to potential overseers, too, since they are to be culled from the best of the auxiliaries, although, as we will see, overseers require additional education.) The curriculum breaks down into gymnastic and what Plato calls music (376e). Gymnastic refers to training of the body, and what Plato says about it is not too difficult to follow. We need note only that he regards gymnastic as nothing good in itself. Its real purpose is to serve the good of the soul.

Plato uses the term *music* in a much broader sense than we do, although exactly what he intends the term to cover is not certain. It includes lyric poetry sung to music, but it seems to embrace more. One translator suggests that the term includes "poetry and stories, as well as music proper" (Grube, 1992, p. 33), and another says it covers "poetry and letters and things intellectual" (Rouse, p. 174). For our purposes we can settle on what today we call arts and letters, or the arts, which include music, painting, the performing arts, poetry, fictional prose, and even some nonfictional prose.

Plato believes that arts and letters have a profound impact on shaping character and that therefore they must be strictly regulated. Although the immediate context of the discussion is the education of potential auxiliaries, Socrates extends censorship even to embroidery, houses, furniture, and other output of the craftspeople (410a–b). Socrates' call for banishing poets from the city, in Book X, also makes it clear that the vast system of regulation applies to adults as well as children.

The restrictions Plato puts on the topical content of the arts follow from his idea that the function of art is to provide good models for people to emulate. Thus, tales about murderous, deceitful, and promiscuous gods are outlawed. Plots cannot show evil winning out over good. Stories reporting that war heroes experience fear of death are hardly the thing for future warriors and are accordingly prohibited. Even tales that have gods or humans delighting in frivolous laughter must be kept out of the city. What holds for stories and tales also applies to the other arts, such as painting.

Socrates contends that style must follow content and is also subject to censorship, since how things are said is as important as what is said. Not only must the lyrics of a song, for example, be about good things and good persons, but the melody and rhythm must evoke calm, order, and harmony. It goes without saying that most rock and roll, not to mention speed metal, hip-hop, and rap, would have no place in Plato's ideal city.

Some of Socrates' remarks on style might strike you as obscure. For example, he distinguishes between two styles of narration, reporting and imitation, and is very critical of the latter (392c–398b). A closer look at this distinction, however, brings into sharper focus Plato's conception of art and the reasons he believes it must be censored.

Authors who use what Plato calls the simple narrative or reporting style, even if it is fiction, speak or write in the same general style that we encounter today in newspapers and history textbooks. The speeches and actions of others are reported from the third-person point of view. The author assumes the identity of a narrator and reports, for example, that Mrs. Smith said such and such and that Tommy then did so and so. We never lose sight of the narrator, and we never confuse the point of view of the narrator with the points of view of the characters on which he or she reports.

In the imitative style of narration, on the other hand, what a person says and does is not just reported but imitated. Most of what we encounter in fiction and drama today is in this style. The author disappears behind the events narrated and writes or speaks as if he or she is identical with the persons who appear within the narrative. What Mrs. Smith says is represented from her own, first-person point of view. The author hides (393d), becoming only a transparent medium, Socrates says; the narrator omits his "words between the speeches and leaves the speeches by themselves" (394b).

Socrates suggests that all literature uses some of both styles of narration, but he argues that most literature imitates indiscriminately and resorts to reporting only when absolutely necessary. Authors imitate the speeches of good and bad persons alike and of all manner of persons, from blacksmiths to rowers on ships. Poets even try to imitate "neighing horses, bellowing bulls, roaring rivers, the crashing

sea, thunder, or anything of that sort" (396b). The poet does not simply report that it thundered but tries to imitate thunder, perhaps by
using words whose utterance captures something of the actual
sound of thunder, or by juxtaposing words in a rhythmic sequence
that mimics the roll of thunder.

In good literature, Socrates contends, narrators imitate worthy and
good persons only. They are not afraid of representing good speak-
ers and actions as if they were actually their own. They assert themselves, however, when it comes to bad persons. The speeches and
actions of bad persons must be reported, since to imitate them and
assume their point of view would be to honor them and leave the
audience without a clue as to what is really good and bad. Imitation,
as the saying goes, is the sincerest form of flattery. Also, to expend
the effort to imitate bad persons, to really get inside them, so to
speak, would be to risk becoming like them. As for the imitation of
blacksmiths, rowers, bellowing bulls, or the crashing of thunder—
none of this has any place at all in good literature.

It may be that today the pervasive influence of television, rather
that modern poetry and theater, is equivalent to the role that poetry
and drama played in Greek culture. Much of what appears on television exhibits what Plato calls the imitative style. The narrators—the
writers, producers, and directors of television shows—disappear
behind the scene; we hear and see only the characters on the screen
and not the writers, producers, and directors who created them. To
get to the bottom of Plato's complaint about the imitative style, we
can consider the current debate about the nature and influence of
television.

All manner of persons and situations are imitated on television:
working-class, wealthy, and single-parent families; carpenters, doctors, and lawyers; police departments, television newsrooms, and
school classrooms. You name it, it is probably on the tube. Some critics contend that many of these shows have the effect of condoning
morally questionable practices, ranging from promiscuous sex to
experimental use of recreational drugs to telling useful little lies in
tight situations. Defenders of the shows sometimes counter that all
they are doing is mirroring reality, without make a moral judgment

on it one way or the other. At other times, defenders say that most shows aim only to give us a few laughs or a good cry; it is merely entertainment, and critics get themselves all worked up about matters that should not be taken so seriously.

Were Plato to listen in on these debates, he would find such defenses suspect. He would contend that the metaphor of mirroring is fatally flawed, since mirrors do not make choices about what they reflect, whereas writers, producers, and directors do. To pluck a lifestyle from reality and amplify it thorough imitation as a possible way of living — and more often than not things work out for the best on television — is to make an approving moral judgment about it. As for the claim that television is mere entertainment, Plato would argue that even situation comedies inevitably send a message about how best to handle problems. Consider the conflicts around which plots are devised: the parents in a working-class family find a joint in their son's jacket pocket and are not sure how to respond since they smoked marijuana themselves in their youth; a newsbroadcaster confronts her latent racial prejudices when her white boss is replaced by an African American; or a bookstore owner has trouble dealing with her overbearing but well-meaning parents. Since the conflict in each episode is always happily resolved, the effect is to send a particular message about how a working-class family, yuppy professional, or struggling middle-class business owner should handle problems encountered in daily life.

Plato's criticism of the imitative style may be that it too easily allows its practitioners to deceive themselves. Try as they might, narrators cannot actually disappear behind their imitations, and they sometimes refuse to face up to this fact and take responsibility for what they have produced. He might argue that writers, producers, and directors are present in their television programs, in the choices they have made about what to imitate. That they choose to imitate some things rather than others is morally significant, and responsibility for those choices cannot be disowned by claiming moral neutrality or declaring that art is merely entertainment. For Plato, all art is morally educative through and through, and for that reason it must be carefully censored.

You might object that Plato does not follow his own rule. If he is so wary of imitation, why does Plato convey his own philosophy in a dramatic form? If his philosophy is a criticism of the historical Socrates, why does he not state that criticism outright rather than portray the historical Socrates dramatically in Book I? If Plato disapproves of Thrasymachus, he should, according to his own rule, simply report the gist of what Thrasymachus says. Instead, Plato imitates the nuances and idiosyncrasies in Thrasymachus's actual way of speaking. The discrepancy between what Plato preaches and what he practices is most glaring, you might argue, in the fact that he puts even what he has to say about the defects of most imitative literature into the mouths of characters engaged in a fictional conversation.

There is really no way to get Plato off the hook in this apparent violation of his own rule. The best I can do is to remind you that Plato may believe he is imitating not so much individuals as he is the method by which philosophy itself initially advances. He might say in his own defense that he is imitating what is most valuable rather than just any person or bellowing bull who happens to come down the street. He is imitating the method for beginning the assent to the truth.

A full treatment of Plato's conception of good art and his acceptance of a very limited role for imitation will have to wait until we explore further, in chapters 3 and 4, Plato's conception of the truth and his account of the nature of the real upon which that conception is based. The role of censorship of the arts in his overall scheme, however, should be evident by now. If one takes seriously the influence of nurture in making us who we are, Plato may have a case. If what we see, hear, and read shapes the sort of person we become, then, if we have an available standard for the sort of person we ought to be, and if the purpose of the city or state is to produce such persons, censorship of the arts would seem to make sense. There are probably some things in this argument with which you agree, but most likely you do not follow Plato all the way to his conclusion. To see why, it might help to clarify Plato's position in light of contemporary standards.

That many people today take seriously the influence of nurture on character and believe that it has relevance for politics is evidenced in many ways. Even in the United States books such as James Joyce's *Ulysses* and D. H. Lawrence's *Lady Chatterley's Lover* were once banned outright. Battles still occur frequently over what sort of books should be shelved in public libraries and what books should be included in school curricula. The Federal Communication Commission, working under the authority of Congress, regulates what can be heard and seen over the airwaves. The debate about what pornography is and who should have access to it rages in city councils as well as the Supreme Court. Movies are rated and some musical recordings now carry warning labels about their content. The National Endowment for the Arts, which funds artistic projects with tax dollars, has come under intense criticism recently for supporting the wrong kind of art.

These issues and policies are contentious, of course. Many of us would probably place ourselves somewhere along the continuum between the view that the government should have no role whatsoever in determining what we can see and hear and Plato's view that the state should exercise very tight control. For example, most of us would at least draw a distinction between what should be accessible to children and what to adults. Children are indeed likely to emulate what they hear and see without discriminating right from wrong, so we must regulate what they are exposed to. Such regulation is primarily the responsibility of parents, but government has a responsibility for limiting what can appear in public places that children necessarily frequent.

Plato would find this argument regarding children unobjectionable as far as it goes. From his point of view, though, there is as much sense in regulating what adults can hear and see since most adults are, morally speaking, perpetual children. They are by their nature ill-equipped to discern what is right and wrong according to the truth, so the determination must be made for them by the few who are equipped to do so. Here, I suspect, is where most moderns dissent from Plato's position.

Even those of you who agree with Plato that art is serious business, laden with moral responsibility, would probably not agree to his call for strict censorship of material available to adults. Art may be a moral enterprise at bottom, but, you may object, what gives Plato and other philosophers the right to define *the* standard of good art and moral responsibility? You may feel considerable skepticism as to whether there is a single standard. Or you might hold that there is a single standard but feel mistrustful of persons who dare to claim actual knowledge of what it is. You might argue that we have not arrived at such knowledge, either individually or collectively, and that toleration of competing conceptions of the truth is the very condition for its discovery. We must allow for a free marketplace of ideas in which true ones will win out over false ones.

Plato's contention that philosophy makes its journey toward the truth through a pitting of speech against speech seems to be a way of calling for a free marketplace of ideas. Plato apparently believes, however, that he and perhaps some other genuine philosophers have already arrived at the truth, in which case the free marketplace of ideas can be closed down. While Plato may have used the dialogical form to honor his conversations with the historical Socrates, which launched his own philosophical journey, his politics indicate that he is willing to shut down dialogue unilaterally.

We can hardly fault Plato for being confident about what he believes and for wanting to teach it to others. If we are to teach anything at all — or, for that matter, if we are to write or even say anything at all — we must have enough confidence in what we believe is right to carry us through the act of teaching, writing, or speaking about it. In politics, too, confidence underlies action. Some laws and policies rather than others must be put into effect, and if rulers are to act, they must have confidence in the choices they make. But Plato's confidence seems overarching, for the political arrangements he proposes in the *Republic* suggest that he believes it is actually possible to discover all the truth there is.

Many modern readers also have a fundamental objection to censorship, however, that unites them and distances them from Plato. If the truth is available, Plato seems to ask, why would people want to live — and why should they be allowed to live — outside the truth? Whereas Plato elevates living in light of the truth over freedom, we tend to consider freedom itself to be the highest value, even if it sometimes means living under falsehoods. We think of freedom as an instrumental value, in that it allows for the discovery of the truth, but also as a good in itself. In fact, even if you hold with Plato that there *is* a singular truth and that it is already available — and even if you believe that *you* already know it, as you might, for example, if you hold certain deep religious convictions — you are likely to argue that neither you nor anyone else has the right to impose their conception of the truth on others. In effect, you value individual freedom more than living according to the truth. Plato might argue that true freedom, rather than just apparent freedom, comes from living according to the truth, but it is just this connection that most of us question. The pervasive opinion of our time is that freedom is a good in itself and requires nothing else to justify it, not even the truth.

THE LIVING CONDITIONS OF THE GUARDIANS

What of some of the other details of Plato's political vision? How might his description of the living conditions of the guardians (416c–422d) make sense from the point of view of his overall scheme? Socrates contends that the guardians should be paid subsistence wages, hold no private property except for a few personal necessities, and share spouses and children as well. If auxiliaries and overseers want to have private land, then they ought to be farmers, he argues (416c–417b). To preside over their own households in the city as if they were little fiefdoms is to mistake their function. Private property and wealth derived from excessive wages will only divide auxiliaries and overseers between and among themselves, and disunity within the ranks of leadership, Socrates says, is the gravest threat to the whole social structure.

When Adeimantus protests that such monkish living conditions are not going to make the guardians very happy, Socrates replies that "we aren't aiming to make any one group outstandingly happy but to make the whole city so, so far as possible" (420b). Here, many students say, is another reason for their objection to Plato. They believe he would have individuals exist solely to serve society, whereas they feel that society should serve individuals.

For Plato, however, individuals will be truly happy only if they live in tune with the truth, and since most individuals are incapable of apprehending the truth, they must play a role in maintaining the social structure that makes it possible for others to discover truth and govern everyone accordingly. Thus, while individuals must serve society, society, in turn, exists to serve individuals. When many of the same students who protest that Plato lacks concern for the individual try to justify the government's right to conscript individuals into the military or require individuals to pay taxes, they appeal to the same general logic. By fighting in a war, I am serving society, their argument runs, but even if I die in the war, I am ultimately serving myself since my way of life would die with the destruction of the society that makes it possible.

The charge that Plato does not care about individuals, then, would ring hollow in his ears. What could be of greater benefit to individuals, he would ask, than the opportunity to live in light of the truth, according to the natural order of things? The root of most students' objection to Plato's scheme is not that it benefits society rather than individuals, but concerns the *kind* of benefits he wants to bestow on individuals. To them, the benefits to individuals of owning private property, earning high wages, and living according to their own idea of the truth are more valuable than living according to some supposed real truth.

The importance of unity within the guardian classes also underlies Plato's suggestion that spouses and children should be shared (449a–464d). If differences in wealth can cause ruinous factionalism within the ruling classes, sexual and familial jealousies are even more dangerous. Thus, Socrates proposes that children be removed from their biological parents to a common nursery immediately upon birth. He devises a scheme for defining generations, in which all children born within certain time periods, unaware of who their biological parents are, will treat each other as brothers and sisters. They will relate to all members of earlier generations as either parents or grandparents and to all members of later generations as sons and

daughters or grandchildren, and so forth. Although Socrates seems to
want generally to prevent biological incest, his formula would hardly
succeed in preventing it. Nevertheless, the purpose of having a community of spouses and children is to turn the ruling classes into one
big family that would be undisturbed by divisive claims of mine and
thine. This is a high price for individuals to pay for the sake of unity,
you might protest; but, again, keep in mind the even higher purpose
that unity serves in Plato's plan.

Although Plato calls for a community of spouses, individuals are
not allowed to mate with whomever they choose. Before looking at
his call for eugenics, or the selective breeding of humans, however, I
want to pause to consider Plato's general treatment of women
(451b–457c). Plato has Socrates contend that women should not be
excluded from the ranks of the auxiliaries or overseers, which is
rather audacious, given that women in ancient Greece fared no better in public life than they have in subsequent societies until very
recently. Plato's argument, in Book V, is that although women differ
by nature in some aspects from men, those aspects are not relevant
to the functions they would perform as auxiliaries or overseers. The
potential to fill these roles is endowed by nature, but it is not linked
to gender, he says, anymore than baldness is linked to the capacity to
make shoes. Some women are not fit to rule, but then neither are
some men.

On the other hand, although Plato argues that some women may
have the relevant basic nature required to be auxiliaries or overseers,
he also declares that nature is always weaker in women than in men.
Thus, he allows women into the orchestra, but they are still
restricted to second fiddle. Also, while giving women some cause for
hope in Book V, Plato elsewhere has Socrates repeat some of the
most unfounded stereotypes of what women are "by nature" (see, for
example, 387e, 395d–e, 431b–c, and 469d). While Plato's treatment
of the dignity of women is half-hearted, this is as good as it gets for
women in philosophy and political theory for a very, very long time.

Let us return to the issue of eugenics (458c–459b). For Plato,
although nature distributes the capacity for apprehending the truth
and for ruling to some and not others through a biological mechanism,

we can nevertheless aid nature by improving or at least maintaining the purity of desirable pedigrees. We selectively breed hunting dogs and horses to improve or preserve certain characteristics, Socrates argues, so why not human beings? Those with the best natures, as proven by their actual behavior, will be bred to the best. If by chance the breeders should make a mistake, the offspring will be demoted to the craftspeople class or perhaps just be left to die.

The overseers will have to control the whole scheme of selective breeding, of course, and Plato recognizes that not everyone will be happy with the mates selected for them. If the decisions of the overseers are to be accepted, Socrates says, they will have to be backed up by what he calls a "useful falsehood" (459c-460b). The selection of breeding couples will appear to be selected in a lottery, but the overseers will rig the lottery to insure the proper outcome. Participants in the lottery may not always be pleased with the outcome, but if they are unaware that it has been fixed in advance, they will accept their lot, believing it to be the result of fate or perhaps the decision of the gods.

USEFUL FALSEHOODS

Plato's proposal for eugenics is not the first context in which he calls for the overseers to deliberately concoct useful falsehoods. Earlier, just after Socrates has rounded out the three-tier class structure, he proposes that overseers propagate the myth of the metals (413b-415d). Citizens of the city are to be told that the overseers are fit to rule because the gods mixed gold into their composition at birth, that the auxiliaries are what they are because the gods added only silver to them, and that the limited capacities of the craftspeople are due to the iron or bronze in their makeup. In addition, the overseers should disguise the rearing and education that allows them to develop their golden capacities; these should appear, not as the result of special social arrangements devised by human beings, but as having occurred deep within the earth before their birth.

Many students are troubled by Plato's bold and explicit call for the use of lies. Is there not a whopping paradox in the fact that this

supposed lover of the truth prescribes the use of deliberately manu-
factured falsehoods in his ideal city? No and yes. On one hand, the
policy seems to fit within his general political vision. Plato wants
people to live according to nature. He apparently suspects, however,
that many persons are not naturally going to accept that the stations
they happen to occupy in his ideal city are the stations they ought to
occupy by nature. The natural incapacity of shoemakers to grasp the
truth includes the incapacity to know the truth about their own real
nature, and so they must be conned through falsehoods into living
according to it. Insofar as shoemakers believe the myth of the metals, they will believe their lot is by nature to make shoes and abstain
from any interest in ruling. The myth confers a sense of legitimacy
on the whole social structure and works to inhibit change and rebellion. Useful falsehoods are lies, to be sure, but they are lies in the service of a higher truth.

On the other hand, Plato's call for useful falsehoods does expose a
paradox. Plato's willingness to lie makes it clear that he does not
intend for just anyone in his ideal city to read the *Republic*. If craftspeople were to read it and discover that the myth of the metals is
just that, its efficacy would be undermined and serious trouble
would be in the offing. Plato's useful falsehoods are only more evidence that he is ready to shut down, or at least severely limit, the dialogue by which he says philosophy initially advances.

FORCE IN THE CITY AND THE SOUL

Plato's recognition that many persons are not naturally going to
accept the positions he assigns them returns us to further consideration of his political scheme as a whole, because there is a detail of
the scheme that is curious for its virtual absence. It may have struck
you earlier that there is something odd about Plato's definition of
moderation in the city as the voluntary agreement of members of all
three classes that only philosophers should rule. We have now seen
that Plato at least has a peculiar conception of voluntary agreement,
since he admits that it will have to be won with the use of deceit and

lies. Mythology and propaganda are, to be sure, powerful forces that to one degree or another legitimize political regimes in all societies, but societies also rely to some degree on brute force to maintain their structure and order. Max Weber, one of the founders of modern sociology, says that part of the very definition of the state is that it is the institution that has a "monopoly of the legitimate use of physical force within a given territory." Does Plato see any role for the use of physical force in his ideal city?

If physical force is to be used, it would surely be applied by the auxiliaries, but Socrates rarely discusses the internal police function of this group. Recall that he first introduces the auxiliaries as a means for conquering territory from other cities and protecting it against outside invaders, and that the purpose of their training is to prevent them from turning on their own citizens. Socrates remarks at 414b that the overseers will have to take care that the city is guarded against both "external enemies and internal friends," but in this passage he mentions power — the sort of power that rests on physical force — only in the context of guarding against external enemies; internal friends will be guarded against by eliminating their "desire to harm the city." In another passage, he does say in passing that the auxiliaries should look for a good place within the city from which they can not only repel foreign invasions but "most easily control those from within, if anyone is unwilling to obey the laws" (415d-e). He also says tersely that doctors, whom he apparently regards as auxiliaries in this context, may have to kill persons born with incurably bad natures (410a). But this is as far as Socrates goes in suggesting the need for using the threat of the sword to keep citizens in line.

Plato seems to want to convince himself that nurture and education — exposure to the truth for the overseers and exposure to some truths supplemented by propaganda for everyone else — will be sufficient to maintain social order. If only knowledge can be wedded with power, he suggests, power can be stripped of its nastier aspects. I suggest, however, that in spite of his near silence about physical coercion, much of what he otherwise says undermines his apparent hope that it can virtually be eliminated. In particular, his own account of the psychology of the citizens of his city makes implausible his hope that everyone will voluntarily agree to be ruled by philosophers. To flesh out this argument, we need to delve into his account of the structure of the psyche, or soul, (434d–444e), because his account of moderation among the citizens is rooted in his account of moderation in the individual soul.

Socrates argues that if his analogy between the city and the soul of the individual is to be helpful, cities and individuals must be morphologically similar; that is, they must have the same basic structure, or form. In particular, since Socrates earlier argued that wisdom and courage are lodged in distinct parts of the populace, while moderation and justice occur in all three parts, he must first establish that the souls of individuals are also composed of three distinct parts.

To demonstrate that the soul has at least two distinct parts, Socrates points to the frequent experience of feeling ourselves being pulled in different directions. We want to do something, and at the same time we hesitate. This common experience can occur, Socrates reasons, only if the soul consists of at least two parts, since a singular thing cannot both want and not want to do something at the same time. Here he invokes what in formal logic has become known as the principle of contradiction. A thing must either be an apple or not be an apple; it can never be both at the same time. When it appears that this general principle is being violated—as it does when we say that the same soul both wants and does not want something at the same time—it can only be because we are confusing parts and wholes. It is not the same whole soul that both wants and does not want to do something, but two different parts of the soul that pull it in different directions.

Socrates identifies the first two parts of the soul as a rational part and a desiring, or appetitive, part. When, for example, we feel the urge to slake our thirst by drinking whatever is in front of us but draw back from doing so, we are experiencing a struggle between our rational and our appetitive parts. Our appetitive part demands that our thirst be satisfied, but our rational part holds us back because the particular liquid in front of us would actually harm us.

Plato makes two points about the appetitive part with this example. First, desires arise without thought and are blind to considerations of

[handwritten margin notes: rationality, appetite, spiritedness = soul]

good and bad. We do not decide to have desires; they simply come upon us without our thinking about them. We do not decide, for example, to desire to have sex. The desire simply happens; all the deciding is about whether to fulfill the desire. Second, the appetitive part cannot judge between good and bad. In effect, it says only "I want, I want, I want" and relentlessly seeks fulfillment in the objects of its desire. The determination of the goodness or badness of the objects of desire lies solely within the competence of the rational part.

Socrates attempts to establish that there is a third distinct part of the soul by reciting the story of a man who, when walking by the bodies of persons who had been executed, cannot tear himself away from looking at the corpses and becomes angry at himself for doing so (439e–440b). The point of this example is a little harder to make out. The struggle between the rational and appetitive parts is not difficult to see; the appetitive part wants to feast its eyes on the gore, while the rational part judges that the fulfillment of such a desire would not be good. It seems that it is the rational part that feels anger and disgust at the desiring part for finally winning out in the conflict. But Socrates says that it is a third distinct part of the soul, which he calls spiritedness, that feels anger, disgust, and indignation.

Plato seems to imply that this spirited part of the soul has a volatile emotional energy that the rational part lacks, and thus it acts like a sort of psychic muscle. The rational part knows but does not do. It calmly judges which objects of desire are good and bad, but it is up to the spirited part of the soul to carry out its judgments and react when its judgments are not carried out. In some passages, Plato implies that the spirited part is naturally allied with the rational part as its executive arm; however, if the spirited part is conceived as a sort of pool of sheer energy or psychic muscle, it would seem that it can sometimes serve the interests of the appetitive part as well. And, indeed, Plato says in other passages that if not trained properly, the spirited part will ally itself with desire rather than reason.

But there is also another ambiguity that arises from Plato's description of spiritedness. In the case of the man who looked at the corpses, the spirited part of the soul put itself in the service of the rational part, and its energy took the form of anger at the appetitive part for disregarding the judgment of the rational part. But what enabled the appetitive part to win the battle against the rational part in the first place? Does the appetitive part have a sort of energy of its own that empowers it to execute or fulfill its desires against the judgment of the rational part, and against the energy of the spirited part when it is allied with the rational part? And if so, what is the relation between this energy of the appetitive part and the energy of the spirited part? As we will see shortly, this ambiguity comes back to haunt Plato in his account of moderation in the city.

Having established that the soul has three parts, Socrates rounds out the analogy of soul and city. The rational part of the soul corresponds to the class of overseers in the city, the spirited part to the auxiliaries, and the appetitive part to the craftspersons. Wisdom and courage, as in the city, are lodged in distinct parts of the soul, wisdom in the rational part and courage in the spirited part. Moderation, analogously, is the agreement among all three parts of the soul that only the reasoning part should rule. And, finally, justice is the virtue of the soul that makes the other three possible.

Now, the question is whether Plato's definition of moderation in the soul makes sense given his characterization of its three parts. Given his picture of a soul whose parts are by their very nature divided against themselves, why should we expect that those parts would come to a voluntary agreement as to which part should rule? More particularly, if the appetitive part is by its very nature bent only on fulfilling its desires, and blind to any consideration of the goodness or badness of fulfillment, why would it agree to be ruled by reason when reason will inevitably judge that many of appetite's desires should not be fulfilled? For the appetitive part to agree to such an arrangement, it would have to be able to judge what is good for the whole soul—a capacity Plato denies it. The more plausible expectation would seem to be that if reason rules, it would not be by gaining the voluntary consent of desire but by relying on the energy and muscle of the properly trained spirited part to keep the desires in line by force. In the language of Sigmund Freud, whose description of the psyche as a house divided against itself is in many respects very similar to Plato's description, we keep our desires in line through repression.

The dissonance between Plato's definition of moderation in the soul and almost everything else he says about the soul carries over directly to his politics, since he assigns individuals to classes according to the part of the person's soul that predominates. All individuals have a tripartite soul, but only in the souls of overseers does the rational part govern. The spirited part holds sway in the souls of auxiliaries, and the souls of craftspeople are driven by appetites for food, drink, and sex (580d–581c).

If it is implausible to expect the appetitive part of the soul to voluntarily submit to rule by reason, it is also implausible to expect craftspeople (in whose souls the appetitive part rules) to submit voluntarily to rule by philosophers (in whose souls reason rules), since such rule would inevitably mean that craftspeople will not be able to fulfill their desires. If craftspeople are incapable of voluntarily submitting to the rule of their own rational parts, why should we expect them to be capable of submitting voluntarily to the rule of an external rational authority?

It seems that, contrary to what Plato implies by his definition of moderation in the ideal city, much of what he says suggests that if philosophers are to rule, they will do so not with the voluntary consent of the craftspeople — and not even solely with the craftspeople's so-called consent won through useful lies — but by relying on the muscle and armed force of properly trained auxiliaries. Plato's ambiguous account of the spirited part of the soul seems to reinforce this idea. The appetitive part of the soul has a force of its own that enables it to fulfill its desires against the judgments of the reasoning part, and that force can be held in check only by the superior force of the spirited part allied with reason. Thus, at the level of the city, politics, too, becomes a matter of meeting force with force.

PLATO VERSUS HOBBES ON SUBSTANTIVE AND INSTRUMENTAL REASON

There is an interpretation of Plato's account of the psychology of the craftspeople that allows it to be squared with his definition of moderation. Since craftspeople do have a rational part to their souls, perhaps it operates at least to the following extent. In effect, the rational part says to the appetitive part, "Look, if you are going to fulfill some of your desires, you are going to have to face up to the fact that you cannot fulfill all of them. If everyone gives free reign to all their desires, most of us are going to end up dead and unable to fulfill any of them. Therefore, you had better submit to some external authority, assuming others consent to do so as well, and agree to abide by its determination of which desires may be fulfilled and which not. And philosophers are as good a choice as any for an external authority."

You have heard this argument before, of course. It is another rendering of the theory of the origin of justice that Glaucon and Adeimantus say most people believe, and which Thomas Hobbes reiterated in the seventeenth century. Since it is also the theory that Plato set out to refute, however, something must be wrong with invoking it to try to reconcile the psychology of the craftspeople with Plato's claim that they would voluntarily agree to be ruled by philosophers.

As I noted earlier in the chapter, Hobbes argues that political society rests on an agreement or social contract among individuals. We come to some agreement as to what kinds of behavior are to be allowed, or appoint a special person or group of persons to make that determination. The result is the state — which may involve one of us, some of us, or all of us — which we agree to obey.

However, there is another element in Hobbes's scenario. According to Hobbes, we recognize in advance that signing the social contract will not magically transform us. We will remain the egoists that we always were, and given the chance to bolt from the agreement that establishes the state, we will do so if we think we can get away with it. So, we allow the state some means of physical coercion to enforce its decisions. For a weak internal check we substitute an external, physical check. We set up the state during a lucid interlude in our stormy social relations, and if the rationale for why we entered into the social contract in the first place should lose its grip on us, the power of the sword wielded by the state will force us back into line.

Clearly, Hobbes does not share Plato's hope that social order can rest on voluntary consent alone. The rational part of craftspeople's souls may be capable of a sort of Hobbesian rationality. Craftspeople may be capable of seeing the necessity of submitting to some external authority, but that same Hobbesian rationality emphatically suggests that such an authority could not succeed in ruling without relying on physical force.

Underpinning the differences between Plato and Hobbes are two very different conceptions of reason. For Hobbes, as for many modern philosophers, reason is purely instrumental; that is, it does not provide us with ends or purposes but only the means for reaching those ends. Desires tell us what we want, and reason tells us how to get it. For Plato, too, reason has an instrumental function. However, he believes that reason also has a substantive aspect. Reason tells us not only how to go about getting what we want but also what we should want in the first place if we are to live according to the natural order of things. Reason tells us what we really want according to our true nature.

For Hobbes, our desire is to survive, and our reason tells us that to do so we must submit to an external authority. There is nothing rational about that external authority itself. It allows us to survive because it has the brute physical power to resolve conflict and not because it correctly determines what we want according to our true nature. For Plato, most of us must submit to an external authority not just to survive but because only that authority, the reason of philosophers, is capable of telling us what we really want. The craftspeople, however, would be unlikely to submit to the rule of the philosophers on such grounds. They might submit to an external authority if doing so enabled them to fulfill some of their desires, even if it entailed sacrificing a few of them, but they would not submit to an authority because it claimed to know what their real desires are.

And, I have a hunch, neither would you. And so we return to the the assumptions upon which Plato's political vision rests, which we will explore in the remaining chapters. If Plato can convince us that he does indeed know the truth about the really real and our nature, and if he can show us how philosophy allows him to know that he knows, we may yet have to swallow our objections to his politics.

Suggestions for Further Reading

Thomas Hobbes's most important political work is *Leviathan*. The famous statements quoted in this chapter are from part I, chapters 11 and 13, of that work.

A great deal has been written in recent decades on Plato's view of women. For a sample, see Diana Coole's *Women in Political Theory*, chapter 2. Her book also includes an account of the status of women in the works of subsequent theorists.

John Stuart Mill's short book *On Liberty* is considered by many to be the most eloquent modern defense of a free marketplace of ideas. Some say the essay is simplistic, but it is a good place to begin a rigorous exploration of the idea.

Karl Popper's *The Open Society and its Enemies* contends that Plato made the first pitch for totalitarianism. The book has provoked a great deal of controversy and many efforts to defend Plato against the charge. *Plato, Popper, and Politics*, edited by Renford Bambrough, is a collection of essays by various authors who rebut Popper.

Plato is not the last theorist to embrace useful falsehoods. Edmund Burke, for example, the founder of modern conservatism, argued that "pleasing illusions" that promote social cohesion and stability should not be disturbed. See his *Reflections on the Revolution in France*, especially pages 78–82.

Max Weber's definition of the state as the institution that has a monopoly on the legitimate use of force occurs in his essay "Politics as a Vocation," page 78.

Not all commentators see an incoherence in Plato's account of moderation. See George Klosko's *The Development of Plato's Political Theory*, chapter 5, for example. Cornford argues that Plato recognizes the "principle of freedom — government with the consent of the governed." See his *Republic of Plato*, pages 119 and 125. See my "Plato on Force: The Conflict Between His Psychology and Political Sociology and His Definition of Temperance in the *Republic*" for an extended discussion of the argument I make in this chapter. Cross and Woozely give a good account of other problems with the analogy of soul and state in their *Plato's "Republic": A Philosophical Commentary*, chapter 6.

3

Plato's Metaphysics: Books VI–VII

METAPHYSICS, ONTOLOGY, AND EPISTEMOLOGY

Plato's claim that philosophers can know the truth is the keystone of the rationale for his ideal city. Since Plato seems to assume that he has already gained access to the truth, we should at least examine the plausibility of his account of it. In this chapter, then, we investigate Plato's fuller account of the real and his explanation of how it is that he knows it. To state our project in the specialized terminology of philosophy, we are going to look into Plato's metaphysics, which is comprised of his ontology and epistemology.

I remarked in chapter 1 that the history of philosophy can be interpreted as a long debate among those holding differing claims as to what is truly real. *Ontology* is the generic term modern philosophers use to refer to such accounts of what is. The term, which literally means "speech about being," refers generally to the study of being, or the kinds of existence and the relations among them.

I also noted that a good philosopher must account for why things might appear as other than what they really are; that is, philosophers must explain how it is possible for us to be mistaken about what really is. *Epistemology* is the generic term modern philosophers use to refer to accounts of how we can know what really is, as opposed to what is only appearance, and of how we can know *that* we know. *Epistemology* means, literally, "speech about knowledge"; it refers generally to the study of kinds of knowledge and their respective limits of validity.

Controversy surrounds how the term *metaphysics* should be used, but I will use it to refer to an overarching inquiry into the ultimate nature of reality that includes both ontology and epistemology. *Meta* means "after," and use of the term *metaphysics* derives from the fact that in an early collection of the works of Aristotle, a student of Plato's, texts that address the ultimate nature of reality come *after* texts that deal with physics. (Incidentally, in Aristotle's works, the term *physis* already has a meaning somewhat closer to the typical modern conception of nature than it does in Plato's works.)

Given what Plato says about the natural inability of most of us to grasp the truth, he might find our efforts to understand his metaphysics to be doomed from the start. If we find his account implausible, he might say the problem lies in our natural incapacity to know the truth and not in his metaphysics. Therefore, we will have to presume that we are among the luckily endowed and are capable of retracing his journey from ignorance to truth. If we fail (and few philosophers even would claim to fully understand Plato) he may think he is vindicated. If Plato is really convinced that our failure to understand him only confirms that we are incapable of knowing the truth, we may have to live with the fact that we will be unable to argue him out of that conviction.

We will be free, of course, to consider from our point of view the political consequences if we find the metaphysical keystone of Plato's theory to be implausible. I will do that in chapter 5, and will argue there that even if we reject Plato's broad political scheme, there is still much we can learn from Plato about our political options. In this chapter, though, let us bracket political considerations and try to understand how Plato arrived at his metaphysics.

While the above definitions of ontology and epistemology, the two major branches of metaphysics, are fairly abstract, there is no reason to be intimidated by them. You undoubtedly already engage in a little ontology and epistemology yourself. For instance, a friend tells you that he is going to buy fifty lottery tickets because he had a dream that he picked the winning number. You might reply that his reasoning is absurd, since dreams are not real. You do not mean that he did not really have the dream. Dreams occur, they exist; but they have a kind of existence that we must distinguish from waking life. Your friend might protest that there is a relationship between waking life and dream life. Perhaps you grant him this point, but argue that dreams, nevertheless, are not the sort of thing to rely on in making judgments about what to do in waking life. For such judgments, you say, we would do better to rely on science, which provides us with more reliable knowledge. In drawing distinctions between kinds of being and kinds of knowing, you are engaging in ontology and epistemology.

Epistemology and ontology go hand in hand. We, the knowers of being, are also beings. Therefore, if we begin with ontology and give a complete account of being, including the sort of being we have, we will at the same time provide at least an implicit epistemology. Implicit in the description of the sort of being we have and the sort of being other things have is an assumption about how the sort of being we have can know the sort of being other things have.

Alternatively, if we begin with epistemology and give a complete account of what we can know, we will at the same time provide at least an implicit ontology. Implicit in the explanation of how we can know what we know is a description of the sort of being we have and the sort of being other things have such that we can know the sort of being other things have. Every theory of being implies a theory of knowledge, and every theory of knowledge implies a theory of being. (Some modern philosophers disagree and think that one can do epistemology without doing ontology. Those who hold this position tend to use the term *metaphysics* synonymously with *ontology* and treat epistemology as a completely separable and discreet enterprise.)

THE DIVIDED LINE AS AN OVERVIEW OF PLATO'S METAPHYSICS

The mutual implication of epistemology and ontology is illustrated in Plato's metaphysics. His most explicit and sustained account begins toward the end of Book IV and runs through Book VII, but it appears in condensed form in his discussion of the "divided line" in Book VI (509c–511d). Since the divided line lays out Plato's complete classification of the types of being and their interrelations, as well as his classification of kinds of knowing and their limits of validity, it provides a tidy overview from which we can start our investigation. Don't worry if there are some things in our first run-through that you do not understand. After quickly putting the whole scheme on the table, we will work through it more slowly.

The first type of being consists of images, things like paintings and reflections in water. The second kind is comprised of what we might call ordinary objects, things like chairs, trees, beds, and human bodies. It includes the sort of objects that, in Plato's view, are imaged in reflections in water and works of art such as paintings. The objects of mathematics and geometry, such as numbers, isosceles triangles, and spheres, make up a third type of being. The fourth and last type of being is comprised of what Plato calls forms, for example, the form of chairs, as opposed to this or that particular chair, and the form of justice, as opposed to this or that particular just state of affairs.

Corresponding to the ontological classification of types of being is an epistemological classification of types of knowing: we *imagine* images, *believe* in ordinary objects, *think* about mathematical and geometrical objects, and *understand* forms.

Plato subdivides the parallel classifications of types of being and types of knowing into two major subgroups. Images and ordinary objects belong to the visible world and are "known" through our sense organs. I put *known* in quotation marks because Plato claims that knowledge through senses is not properly knowledge at all, but only opinion. Mathematical and geometrical objects, together with forms, belong to the intelligible world and are known through the "eye of the mind." Such knowing results in knowledge in its proper sense.

Plato's ontological and epistemological classifications not only distinguish types of being and knowing but order them within a hierarchy. In fact, the specific names Plato gives to the various kinds of being and knowing, which you might find to be a very odd use of familiar words, are less important than the order in which he places them. Plato orders the types of being into degrees of reality: forms are more real than the objects of mathematics and geometry, which are more real than ordinary objects, and ordinary objects are more real than images. As the order of types of being reflects degrees of reality, so the order of types of knowing reflects degrees of certainty in knowledge. We can have certain knowledge only of forms, which are the most real; as the degree of reality of the objects we know diminishes, so does the certainty of our knowledge of them. We could hardly be said to know with certainty objects that have little reality, or that, as Plato puts it, live in a hazy obscurity between being and nonbeing.

This is Plato's metaphysics in a nutshell. Does it make sense? Early in Book VI (488a–489a) Plato gives an account of why philosophers in most societies, far from being kings who pilot the ship of state, are frequently viewed as cranky eccentrics, who perhaps ought to be locked up in the hold of the ship. After reading his metaphysics, more than a few students have come to believe that Plato himself provides good evidence of why philosophers should not serve as leaders. Plato is not only wrong on many things, they conclude, but often talks complete gibberish.

For example, you might object to the whole notion of degrees of reality. Although we can grant that there are different types of being—for example, there is definitely something different about a chair, which I can touch, see, and sit on, and the pure form of chairs—but does it make sense to say that one is more real than another? Or take dreams. Perhaps dreams are not more or less real than waking life but rather a different kind of reality, and we simply need to keep straight which reality we are operating in.

Even if we accept the notion of degrees of reality, you might protest that Plato has stood things on their head. He might be right in saying that images and reflections are the lowest form of reality, but how can some equally ethereal thing such as the pure form of chairs or the pure form of justice, which we can only think about, be more real than an actual chair, which we can touch, see, and sit on? Whatever could have motivated Plato to invent such an upside-down world?

EXPLAINING PLATO'S METAPHYSICS ON ITS OWN TERMS

A good way to examine the support Plato gives for what you might think is a rather crazy view of the grand scheme of things is to follow the program Socrates outlines in Book VII (518b–535a) for educating philosophers. This regimen goes far beyond what the auxiliaries are put through. Even potential philosophers (and, remember, we are assuming ourselves to be such) begin their lives with mistaken beliefs such as the one that the chairs we sit on are at least as real as the form of chairs or the form of justice. The task of education is to disabuse potential philosophers of such common misconceptions. In looking at how Socrates says we are to be educated out of such erroneous beliefs, we will see the sort of evidence that Plato marshals in behalf of his own view.

Socrates begins by directing our attention as potential philosophers to something strange about the knowledge we gain through the senses. Suppose you ask me if my index finger is short or long. I am about to answer when a quandary arises. What do you mean by short or long? My index finger is shorter than my middle finger but longer than my thumb. This tangible thing I take to be so real seems to have a rather ambiguous status. It is both short and long, and my knowledge of it turns out to be not as certain as I thought. Today, in the twentieth century, we are likely to chuckle and announce triumphantly that, of course, the length of my finger is relative to what it is measured against — everything is relative. But Plato would reply that that is just his point. The things we know through our senses are indeed relative, and our knowledge of them is accordingly ambiguous and far from absolute.

Nevertheless, education must begin at the level of the students, and there is still something about index fingers that Socrates can use to direct our attention to another kind of being and knowing. He says that when we talk about shortness and longness, we are talking about length and ultimately about number, or pure quantity, and these things provoke the mind into action in a way that the mere sight of an index finger does not. Socrates contends that mathematics is the science of quantity itself and argues that the education of philosophers really gets rolling with the study of this science (522c-526c).

Mathematics is not without its own peculiarities. We first learn to count, add, subtract, multiply, and divide by playing around with things like marbles and coins, but we soon advance to the study of numbers themselves. We begin to study the properties of, not just four marbles or four coins or four humans, but "fourness" itself. We learn, for example, that the fact that four divides evenly by two is quite independent of whether we are talking about four marbles or four coins or four humans. We also learn that we can prove that four always divides evenly by two, not by dividing groups of four marbles or chairs or humans, but only by studying the properties of fourness itself. We could never prove absolutely that four always divides evenly by two by looking at particular groups of four things, because we could never be sure we had surveyed all groups of four actual things. We can achieve absolute proof only by examining the idea of fourness, something we cannot see or touch. We can "see" fourness itself and its divisible properties only with the "eye of the mind." Although counting and dividing groups of marbles or other tangible things are aids to getting started in the study of mathematics, the science of mathematics itself dispenses with such aids.

Socrates says that we should advance from mathematics to the two-dimensional geometry of planes, then to the three-dimensional geometry of solids, or volumes, and finally to astronomy and harmonics (526c-531e). Like mathematics, these sciences, too, are ideal, in that they study objects we can know only through the mind and not through the senses.

Consider Euclidean plane geometry. Recall your first encounter with it in grammar school. You may have laid a protractor over the angles of several equilateral triangles of different sizes and discovered that each angle measured sixty degrees regardless of the size of the triangle. Now recall your next bout with geometry in middle school. You may have played around some again with protractors, rulers, and compasses, but you soon threw them overboard to embark on a different enterprise. You learned to prove, for example, that the angles of any equilateral triangle, regardless of its size, are all sixty degrees; that the sum of the three angles in any triangle is 180 degrees; and that the intersection of two planes always defines a line. And you learned to prove these and a host of other principles without the aid of protractors and rulers. Instead, starting with a few basic definitions and very general principles, you deduced other, increasingly complex principles. The proofs you demonstrated were about ideal triangles you "see" with your mind alone. Just as counting marbles might serve as an aid in the initial study of mathematics, so measuring the angles of a triangle drawn on paper can be an aid in the initial study of geometry, but sooner or later we must dispense with such aids.

Perhaps you are not convinced that we cannot see the triangles of geometry with our eyes. In that case, consider the peculiar characteristics of the starting definitions and principles we use to create a triangle in Euclidean geometry. A triangle consists by definition of three intersecting lines. But what is a line? By definition, it is a series of points strung together. But what is a point? Here we reach a rock-bottom definition. Euclidean geometry defines a point as something absolutely without extension in any direction; it has neither width, breath, nor depth.

Have you ever seen such a creature with your eyes? It is impossible in principle. We can see something only if it has some spread to it, however slight, even if we can see it only through the most powerful electron microscope. And what is the full Euclidean definition of a line? A series of connected points that has length but neither width nor depth. Have you ever seen such a thing? Again, it is impossible in principle. No matter how fine a line we see with our eyes, it always has some breadth and thickness to it. How, then, could we possibly see a triangle as defined by Euclidean geometry when it is built up of components we cannot see? Strange creatures these objects of geometry.

The same characteristics hold for the objects of solid (three-dimensional) geometry, astronomy, and harmonics. Astronomy, for example, studies the motion of heavenly bodies through space. We initially observe the trajectories of the heavenly bodies with our eyes, but the study of the properties of those trajectories is an ideal one. Like the other ideal sciences, it studies objects we can see only with our minds.

Why does Plato insist that we as philosophers-in-training study these sciences? You might speculate that since we are to become overseers of Plato's ideal city once our education is complete, a knowledge of numbers and geometry would be useful in conducting some of the practical affairs of state. Although the principles of mathematics and geometry cannot be proven by examining things we can see with our eyes, they can be applied usefully in manipulating things that we do see with our eyes. For instance, the ability to determine the trajectory of a burning arrow or the strength of certain geometrical forms used in the construction of a fortress would come in handy if we had to instruct our auxiliaries to attack another city-state.

The study of the ideal sciences may have such benefits, but they are strictly secondary to its real purpose (525b–527c; 528e–530c). The primary aim of such studies is to direct our attention to the fact that there *is* a realm beyond the visible world and that it is only of that world that we can have certain, absolute knowledge. To learn this fact, Plato would hope, is to begin to see that the view toward which we are headed is perhaps not really so silly and absurd.

Notice that the stages of the educational regimen for philosophers correspond to the types of being and knowing laid out along the divided line, and that Plato transposes his increasing sense of certainty about our knowledge into a greater degree of reality of the objects we know about. It is through imagination that we have images, but because images are a pathetically inferior type of being, Plato regards imagination as totally irrelevant to the education of the philosopher. The sort of inquiry with which philosophical education begins, such as investigations of ordinary objects like one's index finger, corresponds to belief on the divided line. The study of mathematics and geometry corresponds to thinking and allows us to begin to operate in the realm of intelligible rather than visible things.

THE DOCTRINE OF THE FORMS: REALISM VERSUS NOMINALISM

The final phase of education, the study of dialectic (532a–535a), corresponds to the understanding of forms on the divided line. We already know that dialectic refers generally to the pitting of speech against speech, but exactly how dialectic operates, and precisely what forms dialectic can deliver are not so easy to understand. Here our effort to follow Plato is going to get considerably tougher, but let's begin with the notion of the forms.

We have already been dealing with what Plato means by forms in our discussion of mathematics and geometry. I referred to these sciences as *ideal* sciences because their objects, which can be seen only with the eye of the mind, are ideas. Recall, for example, the idea of fourness or the idea of a triangle that is built up in Euclidian geometry from points that have no extension. Since the Greek word *eidos* is sometimes translated as "idea" and sometimes as "form," we can also say that mathematics and geometry are *formal* sciences. In studying quantity itself, mathematics investigates the form of quantity rather than particular things that we can count and measure. Geometry studies the form of lines, triangles, and spheres, rather than particular things which are linear, triangular, and spherical. In effect, geometry studies the form of spatiality itself rather than particular things in space. (We saw in chapter 1 that the term *empirical* is sometimes used in a gross way to distinguish the sciences, which address facts, from normative inquiry, which addresses values. It should now be apparent, however, that if *empirical* is used in the narrow sense of referring to knowledge that is derived through the senses, not all sciences are empirical. Like chemistry and biology, mathematics and geometry do not address values and so are nonnormative, but only chemistry and biology are empirical sciences in the narrow sense of the term.)

Plato argues that just as there is a form of triangularity that exists apart from all particular triangular things, there are forms for chair, red, human, beauty, justice, and so forth that exist apart from all particular chairs, red things, humans, beautiful things, and just states of affairs; there is chairness, redness, humaness, beauty, and justness (475e–480a, 596a–b). Dialectic, it seems, delivers knowledge of some important forms that mathematics and geometry leave out.

Plato argues that forms give particular things their being and also allow us to recognize particular things as what they are. Consider, for example, the case of chairs. There are many different chairs: kitchen chairs, padded recliners, office chairs, church pews, folding lawn chairs, and more. What is it that enables us to recognize all these objects, in spite of their differences, as chairs? It cannot be the number of legs they have, since some chairs have four legs, some have three, and still others, such as padded recliners, can hardly be said to have legs at all. Nor can it be the amount of padding they have, since some have padding and others do not. Likewise, it cannot be their color. Even the proposition that a chair is something you sit on is problematic, since there are some chairs, like the backless chairs for computer users, that one kneels in as much as one sits on them. Furthermore, when I go fishing I often sit on a rock, and when I teach I frequently sit on the table at the front of the room. I have also sat on the hood of my car when talking to my neighbor. But I call a rock a rock, a table a table, and a car hood a car hood.

Plato argues that we are able to recognize chairs as chairs, in spite of the differences between particular chairs, and in spite of the similarities between chairs and other things, because there is a pure essence of chair or pure chairness, so to speak, that preexists any particular chair and that particular chairs "participate" in. The "participation" of particular chairs that we see with our eyes in chairness is both what causes them to be chairs, rather than something else, and — because we know pure chairness with our minds (just as we know Euclidean triangularity with our minds) — what allows us to recognize them as chairs.

What Plato calls forms many subsequent philosophers call *universals*, but many of these same philosophers have contested Plato's claims about forms or universals. Plato believes forms preexist the particular things that "participate" in them. He believes universals are not just characteristics abstracted in thought from particular things but are real in their own right. (For this reason "form" rather than "idea" is the preferred translation of *eidos*. To translate *eidos* as "idea" may imply that the *eidos* chairness is created by the mind. For Plato, we know chairness with the mind alone, but it is not the creation of the mind.) This doctrine of Plato's is known as *realism*. The term has many other meanings in philosophy, which we cannot get into here, but in the present context it is distinguished from the opposing doctrine *nominalism*. Proponents of nominalism believe that universals are only general names. They contend that *chair*, for example, is simply the general name we give to a class of particular things. The term *chair* exists as a name, to be sure, but it does not refer to some pure form that has a being of its own in a realm that exists apart from the realm of the many existing particular chairs.

Even Aristotle, Plato's student, had difficulty with Plato's doctrine of the forms. It might make sense, he argues, if we knew what it meant for a particular thing to "participate" in the universal that, according to Plato, makes it the thing it is. But the notion of participation is not very clear. Plato seems to think that the realm of the forms explains the diversity of particular things in the world we live in, and that it is the reality of the forms that gives determinate reality to the particular things that participate in them. Aristotle argues that this is a strange explanation, since the only thing it accomplishes is to duplicate in the realm of the forms the world we live in.

Here is an example to illustrate Aristotle's criticism. Plato would treat chairness as a form that green chairs, four-legged chairs, and red four-legged chairs alike participate in. But what of the color green? There are many different shades of green, but we call all of them green. According to Plato's argument there would have to be a pure form greenness. But what of the subgroup of greens we call olive? There are many shades of olive, but since we recognize all of them as olive, there must be a pure form oliveness. We could make the same argument about four-leggedness. Since there are chairs with four round legs and other chairs with four square legs, and so on, there must be a form four-leggedness. According to Plato, the pale, olive-green chair with four round legs that we have in this world is the particular thing it is because there is pale-olive-green-four-round-legged-chairness in the realm of the forms. A peculiar explanation, Aristotle says, since it would seem that the being and diversity of the forms are as much in need of explanation as the being and diversity of the particular things that Plato intends the forms to explain.

Aristotle's criticisms of Plato's doctrine did not put an end to the matter. Subsequent realists argued that when nominalists treat universals as general names, they miss the crucial point at issue. We obviously do group many things under the name *chair*, but the key question is how we know what things to include under that name. How do we know, for instance, when to apply the name *chair* to some particular object we have never seen before. It will not help to look at the list of particular things we already include under the name *chair* if this new thing has features that none of the other things do. There must be, realists argue, some universal essence of chair that is not simply an after-the-fact name for a list of things that share certain features; rather, there is some criterion that allows us to determine what things do or do not go on the list in the first place.

Some recent nominalists counter by arguing that we learn to apply names correctly through usage; and correct usage, they say, is a matter of what works in our efforts to communicate rather than a matter of checking to see if a particular thing participates in an unchanging, universal essence. Anything on the list of things we call *chair* will share some features with some other things on the list, but there is no single, unchanging feature shared by all the particular chairs. There are only loose "family resemblances." One chair may have four legs and another three, but both may have padded seats and backs. Another may have padded seats and backs but no legs. Yet another may have no legs, a padded seat, and no back. And so on.

This means that names refer to lists that are fuzzy at the edges. There is no hard and fast way to tell if we are using the name *chair* properly; only slow-changing usage can serve as our guide. If I want to tell my neighbor I am going to have a mechanic oil the hinges on the thing that covers the engine of my car, I say *car hood* rather than *chair*, not because this thing shares in an unchanging, essential car-hoodness rather than an unchanging, essential chairness, but because my neighbor will get very confused if I say *chair*. The reason she will get confused is that she has never heard anyone else call the things that cover car engines *chairs*. And I will say *car hood,* rather than *chair*, even if I am sitting on the thing that covers my car engine when I am talking about it. If for some reason many people began to sit a lot more frequently on a great variety of occasions on the things that cover their car engines, a few persons might well begin to call these things *chairs.* There would be some initial confusion, but if other persons picked up the practice, we would eventually call the things that cover our car engines *chairs*—and successfully communicate—as unthinkingly as we now apply the name to the things we sit on when we eat dinner.

Defenders of Platonic realism find problems in even this argument, but I am going to leave the general debate between realists and nominalists at this point, for even if it is resolvable at the level of chairs, horses, and olive greens, such a resolution will not help us much when it comes to the forms of things that matter most to Plato. If dialectic is to address matters such as justice and how we ought to live, it must help us understand more than just chairness and tableness. And according to Plato it does; through dialectic we can discover such things as the form of justice and the form of the good.

DIALECTIC AND THE FORM OF THE GOOD

As we have seen, the forms are at the top of a hierarchy that includes other, inferior types of being. There is also a hierarchy among the forms themselves. In fact, Plato contends that even the form of justice, which preexists any particular just thing or just state of affairs, is subordinate to a higher form, the form of the good (504a–508b). Here we arrive at the concept of Plato's that is most difficult to comprehend. It is so, in part, because Plato says himself that he can only speak about the form of the good indirectly and metaphorically.

What he does say is that just as chairness is a form in which all particular chairs participate, goodness is a form in which all particular good things or states of affairs participate. And just as the reality of chairness both causes particular chairs to be what they are and (as a thing known by the mind) allows us to recognize particular chairs we see with our eyes as chairs, so the reality of goodness both causes particular good things to be what they are and allows us to recognize particular good things as good. However, the form of the good causes not only particular good things to be what they are but all other things as well, including, apparently, the lesser forms such as chairness, triangularity, and even the form of justice.

Using an analogy drawn from the world of visible things, Socrates asks us to think of the sun, the light of which provides the energy that causes all other things to grow as well as the means by which we can see them. The form of the good, he says, is like the sun. All other things, including ourselves, exist because of the form of the good, and we can know these other things — which include triangles and triangularity, chairs and chairness, justice and the form justice, as well as the form of the good itself — only because of its "light."

The allegory of the cave in Book VII (514a–521c) also illustrates the place of the form of the good at the top of Plato's ontological hierarchy. Most of us, Socrates says, are like prisoners chained before a wall in a cave, unable to turn our heads. What we call reality is actually a mere shadow play on the wall, projected from behind our backs by persons carrying statues of humans and animals and carved likenesses of other ordinary objects before a fire that is behind them. Philosophers who achieve knowledge of the form of the good are like prisoners who have broken their chains and made their way up and out of the cave into the sunlight. There they see just how far removed from reality they previously were. In the cave, they knew only shadows of what were only copies of ordinary objects; in the light of the sun they are able to see the objects themselves and finally the sun itself, which gives being to all else.

Plato's disparagement of art is also based on his ontological hierarchy. The painting of a bed or table, he says at the beginning of Book X, where he returns to a discussion of art, is at least two steps removed from reality (595a–597e). The form of the bed is the truly real, the beds crafted by carpenters and on which we sleep are imitations of the form, and the painting of the bed is an imitation of an imitation. Since the form of the good is that which gives being to lesser forms, the painting is three steps removed from the highest kind of reality. This is the root of Plato's objection to art and its imitative style, the reason it barely qualifies as even a first rung on the ladder to truth and is irrelevant to the education of philosophers.

Plato treats the form of the good, then, as a final and highest reality upon which all other things are dependent. It is a sort of cause of all causes; without knowledge of goodness our knowledge of other things is uncertain. Socrates contrasts knowledge of the form of the good with knowledge of mathematics and geometry in terms of their respective certainty as well as their respective objects. While I said previously that geometry and mathematics constitute absolute knowledge, Plato would have me qualify this statement. In geometry, for example, we can prove with certainty highly complex principles involving triangles setting out from a few simple definitions of points and lines and principles such as "parallel lines never meet." But what of these beginning definitions and principles? Since we must take these for granted as unproven assumptions, geometry can generate only relatively absolute knowledge.

By contrast, Plato says, dialectic culminating in understanding of the form of the good produces absolutely absolute knowledge (510b–511d). He argues that whereas mathematics and geometry make their way from assumed and unproven beginning hypotheses to conclusions that are only as certain as those hypotheses, dialectic makes only temporary use of hypotheses to work its way back to the unassumed beginning of all beginnings: knowledge of the form of the good. Socrates describes hypotheses as temporary stepping stones. To use another metaphor, we might say that dialectic allows us to hoist ourselves into the air with the help of scaffolding and then throw the scaffolding away. In achieving knowledge of the cause of all causes, we also achieve knowledge of the cause of our being able to know the cause of all causes, and thus we arrive at truly presuppositionless knowledge.

PROBLEMS IN PLATO'S METAPHYSICS INTERPRETED ON ITS OWN TERMS

What are the provisional hypotheses from which dialectic starts out, and how exactly does a pitting of speech against speech lead to the discovery of a form of goodness that is independent of all particular good things? Plato's text raises more questions than it answers. It seems that the beginning hypotheses are statements about particular good things and that through argument we distill the essence of goodness by progressively eliminating from particular good things any attributes that vary from thing to thing. The debate in the dialectic is about what is particular and what is universal in good things; we want to find only what does not vary, or what is universal to all good things. But how do we know when we have succeeded? How do we know, and how do we know that we know, when we have actually arrived at the universal essence of goodness? How do we know that we are not mistaking what might be merely common to the particular good things we have surveyed for what is truly universal? Plato sometimes implies that knowledge of our success will occur as a sort of revelation that finally forces itself upon us, a mystical experience that carries proof of its validity within itself. But this description assumes more than it explains.

Furthermore, is there really anything left to goodness after we eliminate from it all the characteristics that vary among particular things that are good? More specifically, is there anything left that is even remotely relevant to politics or the everyday lives of human beings? Recall that Plato wants a standard for how we ought to live that transcends *nomos*, that gets beyond standards based on convention, custom, and habit, which can vary from society to society. Plato seems to assume that because we still have things to say about triangles once we eliminate from them everything that is unique to particular triangles, we will still have things to say about goodness when we eliminate from it everything that is unique to particular good things. But are triangularity and goodness similar enough for this assumption to be valid?

Had Plato informed us of the content of the form of the good he claims to have seen, we might be able to test this assumption. Presumably Plato knows that everything he asserts in the *Republic* is true because he has seen how it emanates from the true cause of all causes. He supposedly knows that he has hit upon the true form of justice (sticking to the tasks assigned to one by nature), for example, because he has seen how it derives from the even higher form of the good. But although Plato assures us that it derives from the form of the good, he does not tell us how it so derives. To do that he would have to fill us in more on the content of the form of the good, but on this matter, the keystone that holds his entire metaphysics together, Plato is strangely silent.

Perhaps it is unfair to ask to know the content of a form, since we usually use these terms in contradistinction to each other. Form, when pure, has no content. Then again, maybe it is illusory to think that we can ever completely separate form from content. If we can separate it, as Plato seems to believe, but we cannot describe pure form, then we are back to the question of relevance, since it is difficult to see how something we cannot speak about can function as a useful standard for how we ought to live.

Many artists claim that they, too, are after universals; and those who see art as having a moral purpose might claim they are out to depict goodness. But artists usually argue that they can get at the universal only through the particular. The painter who refuses to paint with particular colors and particular shapes will cease to paint. The poet who refuses to use the words of a particular language, which are imbued with particular connotations, will cease to write. Although Plato seems to think dialectic must pass through particulars, he also seems to believe that it can finally succeed in apprehending the form of the good without any mediating particularity. Dialectic initially operates through speech, but it seems to culminate for Plato in a connection with the form of the good that is unburdened even by the particularity of language. What such an apprehension might be we can only wonder.

INTERPRETING PLATO'S METAPHYSICS
FROM OTHER POINTS OF VIEW:
ACKNOWLEDGING FINITUDE

So far I have been attempting to explain Plato's metaphysics on its own terms. This approach, as we have seen, has its limitations. Plato would probably not be surprised; he would claim that my failure to understand his point of view is simply a mark of my own natural inability. I am going to turn the table now: Just as Plato is presumptuous enough to think that he can explain me from his own point of view, I will do the same and interpret him from other perspectives. If we cannot make sense of Plato's metaphysics on its own terms, we can appeal to other points of view.

The sociology of knowledge offers one such strategy of interpretation. Plato was born to a well-connected family, and many of his relatives and friends were important political players in Athens. Their privileged positions and power were threatened, however, when Athens turned democratic. Thus, one might argue, it is easy to understand why Plato would find attractive a metaphysics that demonstrates democracy to be unnatural and underwrites the claim that only a few specially endowed and trained persons, who can see the form of the good, are fit to rule. The fact that Athens was in one of its democratic phases when his friend and teacher Socrates was executed only deepened Plato's commitment to this metaphysics. Plato thus failed to see the flaws in his metaphysics because, conscious of it or not, he had a vested interest in the system it promoted.

Some commentators account for Plato's metaphysics pretty much along these lines. There is probably some merit to this interpretation, as I hinted in chapter 1 in discussing Plato's concern with political stability. Plato was only human and may have been as capable as the next person of unwittingly clothing naked self-interest in the guise of the "truth of nature." However, such an interpretation does not cut deeply enough. I have been arguing all along that Plato's metaphysics has political implications, or, to put it another way, that his politics is dependent on his metaphysics. That is not to say, though, that Plato cooked up his metaphysics solely to support his political preferences. Plato's metaphysics may have had the effect of making him and others like him feel justified in their antidemocratic sentiments, but that fact does not necessarily explain how and why he arrived at his metaphysics in the first place. Remember that Plato hardly describes those who rightfully should rule as living high on the hog! Plato's possible interest in power for members of his class is too gross and too general to be the sole motivation for his elaborate metaphysics.

To get at a more fruitful point of view, let us return to the most troublesome component of Plato's metaphysics, the form of the good. Aristotle further developed the concept of a cause of all causes, or first cause, which is not itself caused by anything else. In Aristotle's metaphysics, the "prime mover" sets all other things in motion but is not moved itself by anything outside itself. Plato's notion of the form of the good, while not exactly the same as Aristotle's idea, seems to play the same role in his philosophy as the prime mover does in Aristotle's.

You will probably recognize affinities between these ideas and the Judeo-Christian doctrine of God as the "alpha and omega," the first and the last, the supreme creator who was not created by anything else. Some critics, in fact, have dubbed Aristotle's prime mover and Plato's form of the good as "philosophers' gods," meaning that although they seem to have some of the same functions as the Judeo-Christian God, they are rather cold and abstract by comparison. Aristotle claims to have arrived at his notion through purely rational deduction. All things that are moved must have a mover, but somewhere back down the line of movers there must be one that is not moved by anything else. He says he came to this idea by disinterestedly following his curiosity. Plato gives us the impression that he arrived at knowledge of the form of the good by following the rational path of dialectic wherever it took him. I do not think, however, that we can take his own account of what it is he is doing and why he is doing it at face value. There may be more going on in Plato's metaphysics than he acknowledges.

If Plato's form of the good functions as a kind of final and highest reality on which all other things depend, a sort of cause of all causes, it can indeed appear to be a rather cold and purely rational concept. But is it? The doctrine of the form of the good expresses Plato's broadest judgment about the character of the real: what is most real is pure, unmitigated goodness; evil has a lesser, illusory status. Such a declaration hardly seems purely rational given that much of human experience suggests that evil is at least as real as goodness. Thus, Plato's ontological ordering of good and evil may not be the product of cold reason and dialectic, as he implies, but rather the offspring of hope. His declaration that the highest form of the real is untainted goodness may actually spring from the nagging suspicion that evil is in fact as real as goodness.

An interesting pattern pervades Plato's thought. Consider the following list of important concepts and their opposites that appear throughout the *Republic*: one/many, unitary/diverse, universal/particular, eternal/temporal, infinite/finite, unchanging/changing, ordered/disordered, intelligible/physical, contemplative/active. The first terms in each pair are related, as are the second ones. For example, too much diversity can spell disorder, diversity increases if things change, and things change in time. Physical things are particular, finite, temporal, and changing. The point is that Plato consistently elevates the first term in each pair to an attribute of what is more real and degrades the second term to an attribute of what is less real and constitutes appearance.

The purported rationality of this ordering of things shipwrecks on some tough, interrelated questions. Plato often talks of the form of the good as a whole that includes everything else as parts, and he maintains that dialectic culminates in knowledge of the whole. But how can such a perfect reality, outside of which there can be nothing if it is truly the whole, produce within itself lesser, imperfect kinds of reality? How can a whole that is fully real contain parts that are not fully real? For that matter, why would the whole go to the bother of causing itself to exist as parts at all? Why would what is eternal stoop to cause, or even allow within itself, a world that is merely temporal? And why would a reality that really is what it is condescend to produce beings who are capable of mistaking what reality is?

I do not see how Plato can provide rational explanations to answer these questions. Likewise, it is not rational to assert that the unchanging, eternal, ordered, and intelligible is more real than the changing, temporal, disordered, and physical. If there is no disinterested and rational motivation behind Plato's scheme of degrees of reality, however, there may yet be an understandable one.

Consider again the types of being that Plato says are inferior to the form of the good but are themselves arranged in a hierarchy. What is it about the things we see with our eyes, such as index fingers, that Plato finds inferior to the objects of geometry and the other forms? Plato argues that they are inferior because they exist in an ambiguous or relative state between being and nonbeing. But does he really believe the things we can see with our eyes only half exist, or do they exist too fully because of their insistent particularity? The visible world can sometimes appear ominous to us because the things that make it up are so very diverse, so utterly particular, that we feel confronted with disorder and chaos.

For Plato, if we are to concern ourselves with index fingers at all, it should be not with short ones, long ones, thin ones, or mangled ones, but with the pure form of index-fingerness. In his vision, to enter the world of forms is to enter a simpler, more serene, totally ordered realm of being, a place where there are no loose ends and nothing is out of place, where everything has an unambiguous function. It is a realm where no thing possesses particularities that would allow it to be confused with another thing, but where each thing can find its home within a hierarchy of ever increasing generalities. The form of pale army green finds its home in the order of olive greens; olive greens find their home in the order of greens; greens find their home in the order of colors; and, somewhere, ultimately, colors find their home in the order of all orders, the form of the good. And so it is with all forms.

This vision is seductive, despite the fact that its rational intelligibility breaks down and that, as Aristotle charged, there seems to be as much unexplained diversity and particularity in the realm of the forms as in the world we live in. Plato himself anticipated, in his *Parmenides*, the sort of objections raised by Aristotle, but, although he could not offer any satisfactory rebuttals, he never abandoned his vision. One wonders if Plato felt the disturbing threat of disorder — felt it as an evil — and, to disarm that threat, convinced himself that disorder is after all not completely real, that the really real includes only what is perfectly ordered.

Another deficiency Plato found with the visible world is that the things composing it do not last forever. They are temporal through and through. Temporality means change, and change means loss; things come to be and pass away. Another philosopher described time as a "perpetual perishing." The passing of time can evoke a great deal of pathos in us. We might accommodate ourselves fairly easily to the loss of chairs and maybe even our index fingers, but the perishing of many other things about which we care deeply is often hard to accept. Plato finds the realm of the forms, by contrast, to be eternal. It is a world without loss, since the forms never change. The objects of the ideal sciences, according to Plato, enjoy the luxury of timelessness. Triangles drawn on paper and square tables come and go, but the triangles and squares of Euclidian geometry were (even before Euclid discovered them) and always will be what they are. Even index-fingerness, as opposed to index fingers, always was and always will be just what it is. Perhaps Plato felt the painful sting of time as a perpetual perishing, and to relieve that sting convinced himself that the temporal world is after all not completely real, that the really real is that which is eternal.

Another key to understanding Plato's declarations about what is real and what is illusory may be the experience of how time ravages our own bodies. As physical things, our bodies are finite, temporal, and changing; they are subject to disease, decay, and finally death. If there is a loss that is difficult for nearly all of us to swallow, it is the loss of ourselves in death. In many passages where he discusses the human body, Plato expresses a sense of disgust, sometimes bordering on revulsion, at the body. Is this because, as he says, he finds the body to be not fully real? Or is it because the body is only too real, because he knows his body will finally fail him? Perhaps Plato felt the inevitability of death to be intolerable and to assuage that knowledge he convinced himself that even his body was not completely real. What is real is the "eye of the mind," the psyche, or soul, which because it knows or is in touch with eternal things, must itself be eternal. To the extent that he could convince himself of this, perhaps it is not so mysterious that he would declare in his most general judgment that the highest reality is unambiguously good.

Plato's arguments about the nature of numbers and universals, although interesting in themselves, can be interpreted as a valiant attempt to buttress an uncertain hope that has little to do with the nature of numbers and universals. Plato's obsession with demonstrating that real knowledge is absolutely certain can be interpreted similarly. It may be less a concern with knowledge in general than a reflection of his ardent desire to believe, contrary to fact, that death is only an illusion.

Plato's metaphysics is not presuppositionless, as he says true philosophy must be, but circular. In strictly logical terms, it is a grand exercise in what philosophers call *petitio principii*, or "begging the question"; that is, Plato assumes from the start what he purportedly is out to prove. This is not to say that all the arguments Plato marshals as evidence for his metaphysical conclusion that what is most real is unequivocally good are without merit. The sort of being that the objects of mathematics and geometry have, for example, *is* quite peculiar. Philosophers still argue about how we should talk about it. Plato sees the odd character of these ideal objects as evidence of their being more real than the things we know through the senses, however, only because he has assumed that what is most real is intelligible rather than visible, unchangeable rather than changeable, strictly ordered rather than disordered. He can see the peculiar character of these objects as intimations of a higher reality only because he has assumed there is a higher reality of which these objects are indicators.

Similarly, the nature of universals is odd. I am not sure myself that contemporary nominalists have accounted for all of their oddity.

Plato can see the strange character of universals as evidence of their superiority over the inferior reality of particular existing things, however, only because he has assumed that the most real must be unburdened by any particularity that cannot be subsumed under ever higher orders of generality.

Plato could respond to these challenges by simply turning the tables on me, however. He could argue that I believe he has made a mistake only because I have assumed that whether a realm of things is ordered or disordered is no measure of its reality. It is only because I already assume that the length of time a thing endures is no measure of its reality that I think he is wrong in equating eternality with reality. From Plato's point of view, it is I who am begging the question.

Apparently no philosophy can be presuppositionless, and all philosophies are ultimately circular in their arguments. Beneath all their technical and logical fine points, philosophical systems express a certain posture toward ourselves and the world. No philosophy can get out from under the posture toward existence that it commends in order to show that it is necessarily the only true one. The work of a philosophical system, then, is not to provide an ultimate proof of what it commends, but to offer as complete an account as possible of what it commends. Since all philosophies are ultimately circular, we can only evaluate them according to how many facets of our experience they take into account and the extent to which their accounts adequately explain our experience.

You must decide which you find more plausible, Plato's own account of his metaphysics or my interpretation of that account. I remarked at the end of chapter 1 that philosophy, originating in the problems of ordinary life, can ironically become a diversion from life and perhaps even offer an escape from life. If my interpretation of Plato's metaphysics as an attempt to find compensation for the finitude of our lives is plausible, his metaphysics offers a good example of how philosophy can take such a twist. The seduction to which Plato falls prey may be the most human of all seductions, but I think we must struggle against it. It is better to try to embrace life in spite of its finitude rather than deny its finitude, even in a subtle way.

Doing this is not easy — in fact it may be virtually impossible — but I think we need to make the struggle nevertheless.

Suggestions for Further Reading

The notion of degrees of reality has a long history after Plato. René Descartes, the seventeenth-century French philosopher and author of the famous line "I think, therefore I am," for example, invokes it in his attempt to prove the existence of God. See the third meditation in his *Meditations on First Philosophy.*

Aristotle's central criticisms of Plato's doctrine of the forms are found in his *Metaphysics,* sections 987b and 990b. He states his doctrine of the prime mover in section 1071b–1073b of the same work. David Hume, the eighteenth-century Scottish philosopher (mentioned in chapter 1) is a modern nominalist. See especially *A Treatise of Human Nature,* book 1, part 1, section 7. Ludwig Wittgenstein introduced the even more recent nominalist doctrine that general names refer to sets of loose family resemblances. See his *Philosophical Investigations,* part 1, sections 66 and 67. Plato's dialogue *Parmenides,* in which Plato anticipates objections to his doctrine of the forms, is included in the collection of Jowett's translations of Plato's dialogues. See sections 130–135.

Karl Popper comes close to relying exclusively on the sociology of knowledge in accounting for those elements of Plato's metaphysics that he finds otherwise unintelligible, such as the form of the good. See *The Open Society and it Enemies,* especially pages 33 and 141–146.

For further discussion of Plato's theory of the forms and the form of the good, see Annas's *An Introduction to Plato's "Republic,"* chapters 9 and 10, and White's *A Companion to Plato's "Republic,"* section 3 of the introduction. Pappas gives a compact summary of the problems in these doctrines in his *Plato and the "Republic,"* chapters 7 and 11.

My hypothesis that Plato was in rebellion against finitude owes a great deal to the work of Miguel de Unamuno, a Spanish philosopher who interprets most metaphysical systems as offering a sublimated form of immortality. See *The Tragic Sense of Life,* especially chapters 1–3. In his novel *Nausea,* the French philosopher Jean Paul Sartre describes in concrete terms the threat of being overwhelmed by particularity that I suggest may have haunted Plato. John Locke is the philosopher who described time as a "perpetual perishing." See his *Essay Concerning Human Understanding*, book 2, chapter 14. The term "philosophers' gods" is Michael Weinstein's; for two comprehensive accounts of the possibility of the good life based on acceptance of finitude in its many guises, see his *Finite Perfections* and *Culture/Flesh*.

4

Plato's Metaphysics and Imperfect Justice: Books VIII–X

THE TYPES OF IMPERFECT JUSTICE

In Book VIII Plato picks up again on the argument that provides the overall structure of the *Republic*. Recall that earlier Socrates sets out to demonstrate that the perfectly just person is happier than the perfectly unjust person, and he constructs the ideally just city as a means of identifying what true justice is in the soul of an individual. By the end of Book IV, Socrates has outlined such a city, identified the four cardinal virtues in it, including justice, and argued that the virtues in the soul of an individual are the same, given the soul's structural similarity to the city.

Having developed a description of the perfectly just person, Socrates begins, in Book V, to construct a picture of the perfectly unjust person. He contends that while perfect justice is of only one kind — its very perfection means that it is complete and unitary — injustice comes in varying degrees. He plans to appeal to the city-soul analogy to identify the gradations of injustice as they appear in large form in four types of cities commonly recognized at the time (445c-e). Before he can even name them, though, he is interrupted and asked to elaborate on the details of the perfectly just city. His response continues through the end of Book VII.

Socrates now picks up at the beginning of Book VIII from where he left off in Book V. He calls the perfectly just city an aristocracy, meaning literally "rule by the best," the best being philosophers, of course. The remaining types, ranked from the least bad to the worst, are timocracy, oligarchy, democracy, and tyranny. The auxiliaries, or at least the generals among them, rule in timocracies; the rich rule in oligarchies; everybody rules in democracies; and tyrants rule in tyrannies. Corresponding to the degrees of injustice in the four inferior cities, Socrates argues, are four analogous degrees of injustice in the souls of individuals. His description culminates in a picture of the perfectly unjust individual whose happiness can be compared to that of the perfectly just individual. The comparison begins in Book IX and runs to the end of Book X, the last in the *Republic*.

Socrates not only describes each inferior type of city and soul but offers an explanation as to how each type is produced. In this chapter we will first look at the rationale behind Socrates' ranking of the various types of cities and souls, and how his proofs regarding happiness are related to that rationale. As we will see, Plato's metaphysical presuppositions are still the key to understanding his arguments. Then we will examine a logical problem in Socrates' explanation of the genesis of the various types of cities and souls concerning the origin of imperfection. Plato's metaphysics is also at the root of this problem. Finally, I will show how Plato's metaphysics sets up a conceptual dilemma that subsequent thinkers, of various stripes, have wrestled with in their attempts to escape the restraints of a finite existence. In the next chapter we will consider what our options are if we acknowledge that finitude.

RANKING THE TYPES OF JUSTICE

Given Socrates' accounts of the ideal city and the soul, it should not come as any surprise that he ranks timocracy as the second best type of justice and oligarchy below it. The key to the ranking is Socrates' claim that each type of city and soul seeks to maximize some particular value. The primary pursuit of aristocracies, both of city and soul, is knowledge; for timocracies it is honor (545b); and for oligarchies it is wealth (550c–d). His ranking of these three types reflects the hierarchies within the ideal city or soul. If rule by philosophers and the reasoning part is not possible, rule by auxiliaries and the spirited part is next best; and if rule by these is not possible, then rule by craftspeople and the appetitive part is the only possibility remaining.

The ranking of the values predominating in the various cities or souls is driven by the idea that pursuit of values on the higher end of the scale restricts pursuit of those on the lower end. Pursuit of the higher values imposes more discipline and order than does pursuit of the lower ones. If one's primary aim is to achieve knowledge, other activities, including the quest for honor and the satisfaction of the appetites, must be limited. The quest for honor is not as worthy as the pursuit of knowledge, but it nevertheless requires sacrificing other values. If it is honor you want, you may have to give up being rich. The pursuit of wealth, a desire of the appetitive part of the soul, is less worthy than the pursuit of knowledge or honor, but even it entails sacrifice. Presumably one seeks wealth as a means to satisfy other appetites, but there will be some limit as to how much they can be indulged if one is actually to get rich. Party too much, and you will lose your job and have no money to party at all. You are at least going to have to pick and choose among the other appetites you want to satisfy. As one descends the scale of cities or souls, there is a progressive relaxation of limitation, restriction, and discipline.

The same principle explains Socrates' ranking of democracy and tyranny, which we have yet to account for. In his earlier description of the soul, Socrates distinguished the appetitive from the other parts of the soul, but he did not discriminate very finely the different kinds of appetites. Now he argues that although the appetitive part ranks below the spirited and rational parts, we can distinguish better and worse desires even within the appetitive part. The first distinction Socrates makes is between necessary and unnecessary desires (558d–559d). Necessary ones are those we cannot eliminate and whose moderate satisfaction benefits us, he says, citing the desire for simple, nutritious food as an example. Unnecessary desires can be eliminated if we do not cultivate them by giving in to them, and their satisfaction is harmful to us. He cites the desire for exotic foods as an example, although were Plato writing today he might cite the desire many of us have for salty junk food, smoking cigarettes, or watching television.

The pursuit of wealth, the driving motivation of oligarchies, requires the discipline to restrict satisfaction primarily to the necessary desires, Socrates argues. What distinguishes democracies is the desire for freedom to pursue virtually all desires, both necessary and unnecessary. An equality of desires reigns, one being viewed as good as the next, and the right to satisfy the desire of the moment is the governing principle. The lack of discipline is almost complete.

But Socrates draws another distinction, this time within the class of unnecessary desires (571a–572a). Some unnecessary desires are lawful, or at least capable of being checked by law and to some extent by the other desires and reason. Even in a democracy, where all desires are viewed as being equal, the very multiplicity of desires checks the obsessive pursuit of any one of them. However, there are some unnecessary desires that are unlawful to satisfy and completely immune to the appeals of reason. Socrates cites as examples the desire to have sex with one's mother, with animals, or even with the gods and the desire to commit heinous murders. For most persons, he argues, such desires appear only in dreams, if at all, whereas tyrants give free reign to them even in waking life. Under tyranny, order and discipline are at their nadir.

You might find Socrates' description of tyrants somewhat confusing, given that he goes on to say that they are most frequently obsessed with love (572d–575a). How can the desire to have sex with one's mother, an animal, or a god have anything to do with love? Plato seems to regard the extreme forms of erotic desire as expressing a longing that too often underlies love in general. The heart of Socrates' description of tyrants as "stung" by love is that they are driven by a frenzied longing for completion and wholeness, for a perfect communion with the beloved that will fill the emptiness that possesses them. Obsessed by this longing that they do not understand, they bounce from quest to quest, doing absolutely anything that is necessary to win the object of their love and are never satisfied. That the objects of their love could include even their mothers, animals, and the gods is only a mark of the desperation of love that demands perfect completion and wholeness.

PROOFS THAT THE MOST UNJUST PERSON IS UNHAPPIEST AND THE MOST JUST PERSON IS HAPPIEST

While tyrants may seem to live with unlimited freedom, in the sense that they do not regard anything as prohibited, they are actually the least free of all persons because they are completely enslaved by their obsessions. Socrates regards this account of the tyrant as the first in the series of proofs that the most unjust of men is the unhappiest and the most just of men is the happiest (575e–580c). To be more precise, Socrates argues that the absolutely unhappiest person would be a man with a tyrannical character who also happens to be the tyrant in a tyrannical city. Socrates makes this connection between city and soul to refute Thrasymachus's earlier contention that it is not any unjust person, such as a two-bit thief, who is happiest but the person who succeeds in being unjust in a grand way. Socrates' argument against Thrasymachus is that the tyrannical character living in, say, a timocracy or democracy, would be unhappy since he would be without any true and lasting friends. He would be forced to sacrifice all friends, and even his parents, to the satisfaction of his obsession. But the person with a tyrannical character who is tyrant in a tyrannical city would be in an even worse situation since the entire city would be allied against him. He could trust no one, not even his personal guards, for they know he would sacrifice them at the drop of a hat. The tyrant is not only obsessive but inevitably an extreme paranoid with real enemies.

Socrates does not bother in this first proof to rehearse why the philosophic character, depicted in the account of the best city and soul that led up to Book VIII, is happiest. In the remaining proofs, however, Socrates brings the best and worst characters back into direct contrast. In the second proof (580d–583c), Socrates contends that each of the three parts of the soul pursues a particular kind of pleasure, just as each kind of city seeks to maximize a particular value. Although he previously treated the appetitive part of the soul as the part that desires, he now says that we can also think of the rational part as having a desire of its own, the desire for the pleasure of learning and knowledge. The spirited part also has a desire of its own, the desire for the pleasure of honor. The desire of the appetitive part is for food, sex, other bodily pleasures, and, presumably, for the wealth that makes these pursuits possible.

Socrates then transforms the question of which pleasure produces the greatest happiness into the question of what sort of person is most competent to judge the matter. Is it the person who pursues the pleasure of philosophy, the one who pursues the pleasure of honor, or the one who pursues bodily pleasures who is the best judge of which kind of pleasure is really the best? Not surprisingly, Socrates says that the person who pursues primarily the pleasure of philosophy is the best judge, and that such a person will declare philosophy to provide the greatest pleasure. His argument is that while philosophers pursue primarily philosophy, they also have tasted the pleasures of honor and the body. Persons who pursue primarily honor, on the other hand, while having tasted the pleasures of the body, have never experienced the pleasure of philosophy. And persons who pursue only bodily pleasure know nothing of the pleasures of honor or philosophy. These persons will be the worst judges, since they can hardly evaluate pleasures they have never experienced.

The rhetorical force of Socrates' argument is simple. If I want to know what kind of ice-cream tastes best — vanilla, chocolate, or strawberry — I would ask someone who has tasted all three rather than someone who has tasted only two or one of the flavors. There is nothing wrong with the argument logically, but, in effect, it only reiterates Plato's entire metaphysics. Socrates says, in the course of the argument, that "the pleasure of studying the things that are cannot be tasted by anyone except a philosopher" (582c). This is the actual operative premise of the argument, and it invokes in capsule form

Plato's ontological statement about what is real and what is only appearance, and his epistemological statement about how we can know the difference. If we accept Plato's metaphysics, then his proof about happiness holds up. If a nonphilosopher said that he or she had in fact tasted philosophy but found it did not provide the best pleasure, Plato would respond by saying that all such a statement proves is that the nonphilosopher had not *really* tasted philosophy.

The third proof that the unjust person is unhappiest and the just person is happiest (583b–588a) is only a more complicated version of the second. Socrates again claims that philosophy produces more happiness than all other pleasures, and he once again supports this claim by saying that philosophers are the best judges of the matter and that they declare the pleasure of philosophy to be best. In this proof, though, Socrates begins by drawing a new distinction between two broad kinds of pleasures: those that are only relative and apparent and those that are absolute and real. Apparent pleasures are experienced as pleasurable only in relation to some prior state that is not pleasurable. For example, if we are in excruciating pain and it suddenly subsides, we are likely to think we are experiencing pleasure when we are really only experiencing relief from pain. Likewise, if we are experiencing intense pleasure and it suddenly ends, we are likely to think we are experiencing pain when we are really only experiencing repose from pleasure.

There are absolute pleasures, however, Socrates argues. Some pleasures simply are what they are and do not depend on a contrasting prior state. He cites as an example the pleasure of smell. A smell comes upon us and is pleasurable without having to follow on the heels of previous pain, and when it ceases it leaves us in no pain. It is a pleasure that leans on itself, so to speak, and is not relative.

Most people, Socrates goes on to argue, are unable to distinguish between real and apparent pleasure. They are like a man in space who in rising to a middle position from the bottom, and looking back down at the bottom, is likely to think he is at the top rather than just in the middle. He thinks he knows where he is, when, in fact, he has no clue as to what is really bottom, top, and middle. His delusion is understandable, but it is only a delusion. Only philosophers are competent to judge what is really bottom, middle, and top because only they experience the true heights, from which even bodily pleasures such as smells, which are thought to be absolute from a lower perspective, are finally seen to be only relative and illusory.

Underlying Plato's account of desire in the third proof is the idea that all desire is fundamentally a lack, or emptiness, that is filled when it is satisfied. Philosophers are concerned primarily to fill the void of ignorance with knowledge, while most persons want to fill only bodily lacks such as hunger, thirst, and sexual longing with food, drink, and sexual activity. Socrates again appeals directly to his metaphysics to argue that the fullness experienced in philosophy is more full than the fullness experienced in the satisfaction of bodily desires. The true knowledge of philosophers is of things that are unchanging and immortal. Nourishment of the physical body decidedly has to do with things that are changing and mortal. Things that are unchanging and immortal have more being than things that are changing and mortal. Therefore, true knowledge, like the things it has knowledge of, has more being than physical satisfaction. And thus philosophy produces greater fullness and more pleasure than physical satisfaction.

CRITIQUE OF THE PROOFS

The general structure of Plato's hierarchy of cities or souls and the accompanying proofs regarding happiness, which assert that the pursuit of values higher on the scale restricts pursuit of those lower on the scale, seems to be premised on a recognition of our finitude. It is because we are finite that to open one door is to leave another one closed, to enjoy one pleasure is to sacrifice enjoyment of another. Like it or not, these are the facts of living in finite bodies in time that passes.

Thus, on one hand, Plato seems to view philosophy as an enterprise that puts before us the limits of our existence; it shows us the order of dependence of things, what things we must sacrifice if we are to enjoy others. This squares, in a qualified way, with my own definition of philosophy in chapter 1. There I said philosophy is an enterprise that develops the reflective component of life into an art form, a project that attempts to give a comprehensive account of life and its complexities. I said essentially the same thing at the end of the last chapter, that under all their technical and logical finesse, philosophical systems are expressions, worked out in some detail, of postures we can take toward ourselves and the world. Such philosophical systems will inevitably include accounts of the interrelationships among the various aspects of existence, and of what the pursuit of given values entails in terms of the sacrifice of other values.

On the other hand, Plato seems to see philosophy as a means of getting beyond finitude — a posture now evident in his proofs concerning happiness. In the second and third proofs, Socrates directly juxtaposes the most just with the most unjust person. The most just person is the philosopher, and the philosopher is the most competent judge of the best pleasure; the most unjust person is the lover of bodily pleasures, and such a person is the most incompetent judge of the best pleasure. But what happened to the rich detail in Socrates' previous depiction of the tyrant as the most unjust person? Where are all the fine discriminations between necessary and unnecessary desires, and between unnecessary desires that are lawful and those that are not? What became of the obsessive nature of the tyrant's peculiar longing for completion and communion? All this seems to have dropped out of the picture.

It does not seem unfair to bring some of this detail back into the picture even if Plato did not. When we do, it becomes plausible to interpret the seemingly strange longing for perfect completion and wholeness that obsesses the tyrant, and that the tyrant seeks to fulfill in love, as the same longing that obsesses Plato's philosopher. The tyrant and the philosopher, finite and mortal as they are, both seem to be seeking communion with something that is infinite and immortal, a communion that will finally overcome their finitude and mortality. Utterly lost to himself, the tyrant pathetically and futilely seeks this contact in love, while the philosopher seeks the same sort of contact through the contemplation of ideal forms.

Plato claims that love has its limits, and it is not just the monstrous tyrants depicted by Socrates, from whom it seems so easy to distinguish ourselves, who forget these limits. Many of us are prone to lose sight of the fact that love offers finite pleasures and fulfillments for finite beings. Contra Plato, I think loving and being loved are the best things this life has to offer, but I agree with him that we too often demand more from love than it can possibly deliver. Rather than recognizing that love must be enjoyed in the midst of finitude, we too frequently seek in it a total compensation for finitude. Furthermore, I suggest that when we invest love with these understandable but impossible expectations, we poison the possibility of enjoying even the finite fulfillments and pleasures that love has to offer. But that is another story.

Plato's account of philosophy, to the extent that it recognizes our finitude, is unobjectionable. To develop philosophy as an art form does, indeed, require great discipline. Like any other art, its pursuit requires a lot of hard work and entails forgoing some other pleasures. It is not that other desires can be denied altogether. Most persons will probably find it difficult to philosophize if they are racked by sexual desire that is never satisfied. And one has to eat and have a roof over one's head just to stay alive in order to be able to philosophize. Like practitioners of the other arts, philosophers should realize that their pursuits depend on the enjoyment of the requisites of mere physical survival. But this recognition is not incompatible with the view that the pleasures of life, while it lasts, can include more than mere physical survival and that one of the pleasures that can enhance life is philosophy.

If these limited claims were the only ones pressed by Plato in his account of the disciplined, philosophic soul, there would be little to which we could object. You may not choose to pursue philosophy as an art, but if you do, other sacrifices will be required, as Plato asserts. But Plato asserts more than this. Rather than seeing philosophy as enhancing a finite life in which trade-offs are inevitable, he views philosophy as an enterprise that finally overcomes finitude altogether and transmutes sacrifices into illusions.

How else are we to interpret his treatment of bodily pleasures such as simple smells? On one hand, he says they are absolute; on the other hand, when he is standing at what he regards as the height of the truth, he devalues them as ultimately illusory. His initial account of smell is accurate and can be expanded to include the pleasures of the other senses as well. For example, the rush of pleasure I may experience in tasting rare roast beef depends on nothing else, on neither a prior nor a subsequent bad taste. It is simply the exquisite pleasure that it is.

The problem is, as finite beings we cannot smell and taste everything. We cannot enjoy the taste of rare roast beef and the taste of sauteed sea scallops simultaneously. We can do so serially, one after the other, but sooner or later our time for tasting will run out. Furthermore, the same roast beef that gives us a rush of pleasure in one moment may also have consequences for other moments of our existence. Eating too much red meat can give one colon cancer, for example. Some persons report that this knowledge spoils their pleasure in eating beef, but these same persons continue to be tempted by beef. It seems more accurate to say such tastes are still what they are, intensely pleasurable, but that they are sacrificed to a competing desire for longevity.

Although physical pleasures may be absolute in the sense that they simply are what they are, they are indeed finite. They last for a limited time and their enjoyment inevitably entails trade-offs. And it is their finite nature, it seems to me, that leads Plato to finally denigrate these activities in favor of pursuing the infinite and eternal, for success in this pursuit, he argues, can show us that although physical pleasures may be finite, finitude in general is only an illusion. It is one thing to recognize that philosophy requires sacrifices; it is another to believe that philosophy can take the sting out of those sacrifices. Plato claims that philosophy transmutes these sacrifices so that they entail no loss, since the pleasures given up are not fully real.

The same twist, in which Plato recognizes the limitations imposed by finitude only to claim to overcome them in philosophy, is evident in his remarks on the inferiority of discipline imposed by the pursuit of anything less than the infinite and eternal. In Socrates' view philosophy does not simply require quantitatively more of the same sort of discipline imposed by the pursuit of wealth or honor; rather, philosophy works by altogether different means. The order imposed by the pursuit of wealth or honor is defective, Socrates says, because it is won through force (547b, 554b-e).

For the person who seeks honor or wealth, the satisfaction of other desires stands as a constant temptation and can only be held at bay by what today we would call sheer willpower. Order of a sort reigns, but it is always insecure. Other desires can be held in check if we do not cave into them every time they arise, but they nevertheless stand ready to break out at any time. Sooner or later these desires will arise, and we will have to struggle all over again to beat them back. The sacrifices entailed by the pursuit of the timocratic or oligarchic life are experienced as real sacrifices that must be made time and again.

The order achieved through the pursuit of philosophy, on the other hand, is won through persuasion, says Socrates, and as such is achieved once and for all time. In philosophic souls, as we have already seen in Socrates' earlier account of moderation and justice in such souls, the lesser desires rooted in the body are not kept in check through the force of will but rather are persuaded to voluntarily cease pressing their demands. By Plato's account, it seems, the lesser desires no longer arise as real temptations, so the sacrifices made by those finite beings who pursue philosophy are not experienced as real sacrifices. Once again Plato transmutes an initial recognition of the consequences of finitude into the claim that we can overcome them. We saw in chapter 2 that Plato apparently had some doubts as to whether the craftspeople in his ideal city would voluntarily cease to press their demands and that he resorted to myths to win their acquiescence. His depiction of philosophy as an enterprise that breaks through the bounds of finitude, allowing us to have our cake and eat it, too (or perhaps convincing us that we do not even want to eat the cake) may be a myth of which he himself was convinced.

THE GENESIS OF IMPERFECTION

Plato was not the last thinker who attempted to deny the finite nature of existence, however, and if such a denial is the most human of all temptations, it should not be surprising to see it expressed in intellectual enterprises other than philosophy. The twists I have been tracing in this chapter were portended in Plato's doctrine of the form of the good, in which he declares that what is wnole, eternal, and good is real, and what is partial, temporal, and evil is illusory. We saw that this doctrine contains a logical flaw in that such a complete, eternal, and good reality could not contain within itself incomplete, temporal, and evil parts that are not fully real. We will now explore how this difficulty is expressed in one further way in the *Republic*, one that will allow us to see more clearly in the next section of this chapter how subsequent thinkers, who otherwise seem very different from Plato, struggle with the same general problem insofar as they, too, attempt to deny finitude.

In accounting for the genesis of the four inferior types of cities and souls, Socrates describes how each kind, beginning with the least bad, evolves out of the kind that is just above it on the scale of justice. Thus, on the city side of the analogy, he explains how timocracy evolves, through a process of degeneration, out of aristocracy, how oligarchy evolves out of timocracy, how democracy evolves out of oligarchy, and how tyranny evolves out of democracy. Socrates follows the same pattern on the soul side of the analogy. More specifically, he describes how a person of a given character type could come out of a home in which the father is one step above on the scale of justice. Thus, for example, he explains how a timocratic man could come out of a home headed by an aristocratic father, how an oligarchic man could come out of a home headed by a timocratic father, and so forth.

Socrates lays out only the general dynamics operating in each case and recognizes that his accounts overlook much detail that would have to be considered in applying them to the evolution of particular historical cities and persons (548c–d). Nevertheless, his descriptions are loaded with fascinating psychological, sociological, and political observations. I will attend more closely to a few of them, especially those regarding democracy, in the next chapter, but for now I want to look at something peculiar in his account of the general dynamics of the decline from perfection.

In drawing out this peculiarity, I will begin at the lower end of the scale. Instead of beginning with the genesis of an oligarchic soul out of an aristocratic one, like Socrates does, I will begin with the genesis of a tyrannical soul out of a democratic one. In the latter account, Socrates considers a son born into a family headed by a democratic father (572a–e). Note, though, that the immediate source of the corruption that drives the son to a lower form of imperfection is not the father himself but the son's other friends. Because the democratic father believes that virtually any desire is as good as another, he allows his son to associate with all kinds of persons, regardless of the desires that drive them, and some of these persons are already tyrannical characters. While the son begins as a democratic character who gives vent only to lawful unnecessary desires, his tyrannical friends will gradually convince him it is quite alright to satisfy even unlawful unnecessary desires. What is odd about Socrates' explanation of the genesis of the tyrannical character is that it assumes the existence of persons who already have tyrannical characters. In a formal logical sense, Socrates begs the question as to the origin of the tyrannical soul; that is, he assumes the very thing whose first appearance he is supposed to explain.

The same pattern holds as we ascend the scale. In accounting for the origin of the democratic character (558c–562a), for example, we are asked to consider a son born to an oligarchic father. The immediate source of corruption, again, is not the father but friends of the son who already possess democratic characters. This question-begging is perhaps not a serious problem until the last level, for one could argue that once there is the slightest deviation from absolute perfection, we are on a slippery slope into the muck of imperfection where logical niceties are beside the point. Once corruption gets its foothold in absolute perfection, the fact that we sometimes put the cart before the horse in our explanations may not be significant. What does it matter when the essential point is that everything short of perfection is corrupt? If this is the position we adopt, it is difficult to understand why Socrates would bother to distinguish degrees of imperfection in the first place. But even if we get around this objection, we encounter an insurmountable difficulty at the next level.

In explaining the genesis of the timocratic character, Socrates asks us to consider a son born to an aristocratic father. Again the immediate source of corruption is not the father himself. This time it is primarily the father's wife, who continually complains that her husband cares too little for honor and money. But here a new question arises. At the lower levels, the permissiveness of timocratic, oligarchic, and democratic fathers as to whom they allow their sons to associate with can be chalked up to their own general imperfection. We can expect imperfect fathers to make mistakes. But how could an aristocratic, philosophic father, with the best and perfect character, ever make the mistake of marrying a wife smitten with timocratic and oligarchic desires? How could he allow his son to associate with timocratic friends? Wouldn't he know the corrupting influence his wife and his son's friends will have on his son, and wouldn't this permissiveness be a mark of his own imperfection? The perfect character, it seems, is not so perfect after all, and is capable of grave errors. Plato derives imperfection not from perfection, but from an imperfection already assumed. Here, at the end of the line, Plato's question-begging has glaringly serious consequences.

Note that the aristocratic father, in whose home Socrates places the son who is to decline into a timocratic character, does not live in an aristocratic city; he resides in some city that is not the ideal one (549c). This situation is not symmetrical with the link that Socrates makes between the tyrannical man and the tyrannical city at the bottom of the scale. Recall that Socrates argues that the absolutely unhappiest man is one who not only has a tyrannical character but who is also tyrant in a tyrannical city. It would seem that the polar opposite, the case making for the starkest contrast on the question of happiness, would be the person who has an aristocratic character and who also happens to be an overseer in an aristocratic city. In accounting for the corruption of souls, the general difficulty Plato has in explaining the decline of the perfect to the imperfect is thus masked, since Plato can point to the city as a whole, rather than to the errors of a supposedly error-free father, as the source of corruption in the son.

The same problem crops up, however, in Socrates' explanation of the corrupt city. In the account of how an aristocratic city declines into timocracy (545c–547c), he asserts as a general principle that decline in all cities results from factions arising within the ruling class. But this only pushes the explanation a step further back, for we need to know what causes factions within the ruling class. In the case of the decline of aristocracy into timocracy, what causes disunity and discord to break out among the philosopher-kings?

In answering this question, Socrates squirms on the horns of a dilemma. One alternative would be to chalk up the origin of imperfection to fate or chance. But this would be to shrink from the task at hand, since appealing to chance explains nothing. Socrates' statement that although his perfect city would be hard to change, it, too, would decline since "everything that comes into being must decay" (546a) sounds as if he is attributing imperfection to fate. In effect, he is saying, "It just happens; this is the way things are." Also, Socrates' proposal that, like the poet Homer, we will have to pray to the Muses to tell us how factions arise, suggests that there is ultimately something mysterious and inexplicable about the cause of factions.

Although Socrates does press on, the other alternative he pursues is no more satisfactory. Like his account of the corruption of the aristocratic man, it comes down to a confession, this time an explicit one, that philosophers are, after all, not perfect. Socrates argues that the philosophers in his ideal city sooner or later make mistakes in their eugenics program and breed the wrong persons to each other, producing future rulers who appear to have pure gold in their blood but who actually have been contaminated with mixtures of silver, bronze, and even iron. Ignorance of the true principles of eugenics, he says, produces rulers with the wrong nature. Persons who should function as auxiliaries or craftspeople end up in ruling positions, competing with those who are true philosophers. Again Socrates assumes the thing whose origin he was supposed to be explaining. He says, in effect, that imperfection arises within perfection because imperfection exists.

More interesting than the logical circularity of this explanation is the fact that it seems to take back much of what Plato says elsewhere about politics. Philosophers, he has argued, should rule because they have true knowledge. But now, as he explains how the first tiny error could appear in such perfect knowledge, he seems to say that philosophers' knowledge is not really so perfect.

Some commentators on the *Republic* argue that there is no contradiction here. They claim that Plato intended his ideal city as just that — an ideal, a model, something to aspire to — and that he never deluded himself into believing any actual city could fully live up to the ideal. By this view, when Socrates accounts for the origin of timocracy, he is describing the general dynamics of the decline of an actual aristocracy, an earthly one, which is the best we can achieve but not absolutely perfect. This is the reason, these commentators say, for Socrates' statement that all things that come to be must decay.

This interpretation has some plausibility. When Socrates explicitly discusses whether he really believes his ideal city is achievable, he admits that it is highly improbable (499c, 502c, 540d–e). But since Socrates also says that achievement of the ideal city is nevertheless possible, this line of interpretation is not wholly satisfactory. The problem is not that Socrates does not admit imperfection of any sort in his ideal city; imperfection is present in the defective knowledge of the auxiliaries and craftspeople. The crucial claim about his ideal city is that these imperfections can be overcome by the perfect knowledge of philosophers. It is their capacity for perfect knowledge that makes the ideal city achievable. The ideal city and actual cities have in common the imperfections of auxiliaries and craftspeople, but the ideal city offers a solution to the problems posed by these imperfections. If this were not the case, if Plato held that the model city is not only highly improbable to achieve but completely impossible in principle, he would undercut its value as offering a solution to genuine problems.

It seems unlikely that Plato would construct his city as a model laid out in the heavens, an ideal we can strive for but never achieve, only to abandon it and begin his account of the deterioration of perfection with an actual and already imperfect aristocracy. While, on one hand, Plato does indeed seem to argue for a sharp separation between the realm of the perfect and eternal and the realm of the imperfect and temporal, he also seems to see philosophers as providing a link between the two. It is philosophy that brings the lessons of the eternal to bear on solving the problems of the temporal. Through philosophy we see how to bring the ideal, heavenly city down to earth.

Whether the contradictions in this vision can be resolved is another matter. One more indication that they cannot shows up in Plato's treatment of the genesis of timocracy out of aristocracy, both in the city and the soul. If at this point he has to confess that philosophers are not capable of perfect knowledge, something is askew in his politics. Would it not have been better to make this admission up front and take it into account in the construction of his ideal city? If even philosophers are incapable of perfect knowledge, would not the truly ideal city, at least one that would be useful as a model, be one designed for persons who are all imperfect?

ACCOUNTS OF IMPERFECTION IN SUBSEQUENT PHILOSOPHY AND POLITICAL THEORY

I will return shortly to argue that the problem Plato encounters in his politics is also encountered by some other political theorists. First, though, I want to show how the general root of that problem — the difficulty of accounting for the genesis of an imperfect lower form of reality from a perfect higher form — also crops up in intellectual enterprises seemingly remote from political theory.

Consider, for example, Christian theologians' attempts to account for the origin of evil. They are compelled to do so since they hold that God is a perfect being who created all things and whose perfection preceded all things, even evil. The question arises, did God create evil?

Their reply is no, that human beings introduced evil into the world. But if human beings are the source of evil, then one must wonder how a perfect God could have created such imperfect creatures. In the standard interpretation of the account of the fall of humankind given in the book of Genesis of the Bible, humans were originally perfect, but part of their perfection included free will, and thus they introduced evil into the Garden of Eden by choice. Choice, however, implies alternatives; and, indeed, Genesis tells us that Eve was tempted by an evil alternative that preceded her.

The conventional Christian interpretation of the fall of humankind goes on to explain that it is Lucifer, a fallen angel, who first brings evil into the cosmos, just as, in Socrates' account of the genesis of imperfection, the son born to an aristocratic father was corrupted by outside influences. But God also created Lucifer, so the problem arises of how a perfect God could have created an imperfect angel. One could argue that Lucifer, like the first humans, was originally perfect but part of his perfection was that he had free will, and he simply chose evil over good. But while Eve was confronted with alternatives, both good and evil, that preceded her, the same is not true for Lucifer. If he was the first tempter, who tempted him? How could the angel Lucifer, as a perfect being with free will, ever have been tempted by the possibility of doing evil? How could a perfect creature have even the inkling of doing evil unless evil somehow preceded him? What was the source of the idea of doing evil? If it was God, then God is the source of evil, even if He introduced it only as an idea, as a possibility that could be rejected. If it was Lucifer — if in thinking the first thought of evil, he brought into the cosmos a possibility that never before existed — then Lucifer is as much a radical creator as God is. Like God, Lucifer is a creator *ex nihilo*, one who brings something into being out of nothing. Neither alternative is logically acceptable, so the genesis of imperfection and evil from a prior state of perfection and absolute goodness remains a mystery.

Now let us return to political theory. Consider two kinds of modern thinkers that seem radically different from each other: "golden-agers" and anarchists. The arguments of golden-age thinkers you may recognize in the analyses of many today who call themselves conservatives, although conservatives do not have a monopoly on such arguments. These theorists posit some golden age of politics during which, they assert, things were as they should be. The state was organized just right, citizens knew their proper stations and functions, everybody was happy, and things ran smoothly. The time period identified as the golden age varies. Some say that in the United States it was the era of our nation's founding, around the time the Constitution was adopted. Others argue that it began at the founding and lasted late into the nineteenth century. Still others contend that it ended with the inauguration of Franklin Roosevelt, when the role of government changed rather drastically. Some even argue that the golden age lasted until Lyndon Johnson destroyed it with his Great Society program. But whenever the golden age is said to have been, golden-age theorists hold it up as the perfect state of things from which we have since declined and to which we ought to return.

The difficulty such thinkers face is to explain how, if things were working so smoothly, politics could have gotten off track. If the golden age was so wonderful, why did things start to decline? Attempts to explain such a decline mirror Plato's struggle to account for the decline from imperfection. Golden-agers either make a vague appeal to some general tendency of things to decay, which is no explanation at all, or, when they try to pinpoint the cause of decline, they end up begging the question. Just as Plato traces the immediate source of corruption of the son born to an aristocratic father, not to the father himself, but to outside influences, so these modern thinkers frequently trace the source of corruption, not to the golden age itself, but to outside influences. For example, alien ideas such as socialism, which some golden-agers believe held Roosevelt in thrall, are sometimes blamed. But if an alien idea started us down the slippery slope of corruption, how could such an idea have taken root in a person raised and educated in the golden age? How could Roosevelt have been so vulnerable to such a corrupting idea, and how could so many other people, whose support was necessary to implement his policies, have been attracted to it if they were so contented and happy?

The point is not that we can learn nothing from past ages, but that the golden age was not really as golden as it is portrayed to have been. The problems that caused the so-called golden age to change and evolve into the situation we are in now are likely the same ones we are dealing with today and for which the golden age had no solutions.

Anarchists face the same sort of difficulty as golden-agers in explaining the origin of our corrupt present state of affairs. Anarchists believe that the good life can be achieved only if we do away with the coercive, formal institutions of government. They stake their claim for abolishing government on the contention that human beings are naturally good. Humans, they say, are inherently altruistic, cooperative, and capable of spontaneously coordinating their activities so that everyone's interests are met.

The first question for anarchists is why, if human beings are naturally so good, do they appear otherwise? Why do they often seem egoistic, noncooperative, and quite willing to sacrifice the interests of others to their own? To this the anarchist replies that the institutions of government themselves, which are meant to restrain egoism and compel cooperation, produce these vices in human beings. The institutions of government stifle humans' inherently good motivations and pit one person against another. Were we to abolish government, our natural virtues would be unleashed and we would live happily ever after.

But there is another question for anarchists: How could such naturally good creatures make the drastic mistake of creating the corrupting institutions of government in the first place? How could such good beings produce such bad institutions? Either this remains a mystery, or, sooner or later, the anarchist is forced to admit that human nature is not flawless after all.

Whereas golden-agers project perfection back onto some past era in time, the typical anarchist projects it in inward to humans' submerged real nature, but the logical structure of the predicament they face in accounting for imperfection is the same. Similarly, the anarchists' recommendations for how we can shed our corrupted outer selves and journey inward to liberate our true nature turn out to be as mysterious as their explanation of why our true nature is submerged. The anarchists' solution bears some resemblance to one of Socrates' proposals for achieving the ideal city. It would be possible to create the ideal city, he says, if all persons over the age of twelve were banished (540e–541a). We would then have a clean slate to write upon, uncorrupted hearts and minds to nurture according to true nature. But who would remain to do the writing? What uncorrupted adults would do the nurturing? Plato's answer is the philosopher-kings. But why, given Plato's insistence on the importance of nurture in shaping character, should we expect philosophers to have escaped the corrupting influences of the old regime in which they were raised? Anarchists have a similar problem in explaining how we are to liberate ourselves from the corrupting influences of government and how those who are to guide our liberation have escaped those influences.

The problem Plato has in accounting for the decline of perfect politics into imperfect politics is structurally similar to the problem that Christian theologians have in explaining the origin of evil in a world created by a perfect God, that golden-agers have in explaining the decline from an age of perfect politics, and that anarchists have in explaining the corruption of an inherently good human nature. Moreover, the logical predicament faced by all of them — and the list could go on, for these are only a few select examples — is rooted in an attempt to flee from finitude. Common to all of these groups' intellectual projects is the hope for salvation of some sort through communion with unsullied perfection. The theologian sees salvation in a return to an Eden that lies beyond this life. For the anarchists and golden-agers, salvation takes the form of political utopianism. Golden-agers seek salvation from the problems of our current state through a return to some past perfect era. Anarchists see a vision of salvation from corrupting government in our natural goodness.

ART VERSUS PHILOSOPHY REVISITED AND THE MYTH OF ER

Before turning in the concluding chapter to address the possibility of a politics that acknowledges finitude, I will comment quickly on the remaining arguments in Books IX and X of the *Republic*, several of which concern the relation of art to philosophy.

In Book IX, Socrates follows the third proof regarding happiness with a metaphor involving a man who has within himself a many-headed monster, a lion, and a human being (588b–592b). The most unjust person is like a man in whom the many-headed monster governs, and the most just person is like a man in whom the rational human being governs. The conclusions regarding happiness that Socrates draws from this metaphor are the same as those he reaches in the first three proofs and are based on the same metaphysical presuppositions.

In Book X, Socrates returns to the question of art and imitation (595a-608a). We have already seen the metaphysical basis for his claim here that art is a third remove from the highest kind of reality: art imitates ordinary objects, which only imperfectly imitate the lesser forms, which, in turn, derive their being from the form of the good. Other remarks in this section only make it clearer that Plato devalues art because it cannot escape the bounds of finitude. A painting of a bed, he notes, is always from some particular and therefore partial perspective. And, indeed, a painting of anything is either an end view or a top view or a corner view; no painting can capture a thing as it would appear at once from all perspectives (598a-598c), from an infinite God's-eye point of view, so to speak. Plato is right about the limits of art, but the contrast with philosophy is specious, since philosophy, too, fails to achieve a God's eye point of view.

Socrates gives tragic literature a special drubbing in Book X (603c-607c). This kind of literature, he says, glorifies by imitating the worst aspects of human beings. Rather than encouraging us to respond to pain and suffering by keeping a stiff upper lip and taking care of business, shored up by the knowledge that pain is an illusion, tragic poetry lets us wallow in our pain and feel good about ourselves in doing so. That a lot of what goes by the name of art does little more than elicit a group throb is still true today. Such art is bad art, but not because it fails to offer a final escape from suffering. It is bad art because it treats suffering in lazy, simplistic, and uncurious ways. Such art functions only to entrench easily earned, hackneyed views. Good art can make us aware of the subtle and sometimes obscure ways in which other people suffer, challenging our comfortable, self-assured views of what causes pain and what does not, and of who the good guys and the bad guys are.

It is difficult to draw a hard and fast line between philosophy and arts such as fictional prose and poetry. It is tempting to say that while both seek to give an account of the complexities of life, philosophy aims at comprehensive accounts, whereas prose and poetry settle for more limited ones. This distinction seems to hold if one compares, say, the philosophical system of Aristotle with a single sonnet by a poet. But if one compares a philosophical system with some of the great novels or with the entire body of work of a great poet, the difference dissolves. We can probably learn as much about life and its complexities from novels and poetry as from philosophical treatises.

Novelists and poets seem to see the fact that we can say or write only one sentence at a time as something positive. This linear approach, for example, allows them to use the element of surprise to advantage. Philosophers sometimes see this same fact as an inescapable burden. They would just as soon get everything out all at once, if only they could, and they often work hard to eliminate surprise. Certainly, the style of most philosophical writing is very different from that of novels. It is not unusual for philosophers to give a forecast of what they are going to do, do it, and then remind us of what they have done.

The philosophical style of proceeding shows the writer's will to be fully self-conscious of every move it makes, and every consequence of every move. He or she wants to be sure that when the work is complete there is nothing outstanding, nothing that has not been brought within the scope of self-conscious understanding. This aim is laudable but it is impossible to achieve. The reason for this is that the language in which philosophy is expressed has a life of its own; words are inevitably loaded with subtle meanings that sometimes say more and sometimes less than those who use them self-consciously intend. Thus, good philosophers should be ready for some surprises when others interpret what they have written. Some philosophers recognize that language sometimes uses us as much as we use it, but then raise this fact to the mysterious and grander claim that language itself is a sort of all-embracing and evolving absolute, outside of which there is nothing else. Typically, they claim to be the humble servants of language conceived as such, but specially anointed servants nonetheless.

After Socrates' final discussion of art, he turns once more to the question of happiness by recounting the myth of Er (608b–621d).

Recall from Book II the stringent terms under which Socrates was asked to prove that the most just person is happier than the most unjust person. The person who is really just but has a reputation for being unjust would appear to be unjust not only to other humans but also to the gods and, accordingly, would enjoy none of the secondary benefits of justice that accrue to a reputation for being just, not even the benefits that the gods might bestow in a life after death. The person who is really unjust but has a reputation for being just would enjoy the benefits accruing to his or her false reputation. Believing he has already successfully demonstrated that even under such conditions the really just person is happiest, Socrates now relaxes the terms of the test under which he has labored. Arguing that the soul is immortal, and that the gods cannot in fact be fooled by bogus reputations, Socrates throws in — as what he seems to regard as merely icing on the cake — an account of the benefits enjoyed by really just persons and the horrors suffered by really unjust persons in a life after this one. Whether this account is only icing on the cake or can be interpreted rather as a sign that Plato may not have been as convinced by his previous arguments as he lets on I will leave for you to decide.

Suggestions for Further Reading

Cross and Woozley are typical of commentators who would take issue with my criticism of Plato's account of the fall from the ideal city. They contend that it is only the order of the various cities that is important and that Plato's account of their genesis is only a "graphic" device. See their *Plato's "Republic": A Philosophical Commentary*, chapter 11.

An early version of the conventional Christian account of the origin of evil in a world created by a perfect God can be found in Saint Augustine's *City of God*. See especially book 5, chapter 9; book 12, chapter 6; and book 14, chapters 11–13. Edmund Burke's *Reflections on the Revolution in France* is an extended example of golden age theory. "The Future of Capitalism," a short essay by the modern economist Milton

Friedman, provides a more compact illustration. Emma Goldman's "What it Really Stands For," in her *Anarchism and Other Essays*, offers a succinct statement of anarchism. Jean-Jacques Rousseau, a seventeenth-century French philosopher, was not an anarchist, but he, too, argues that human nature is fundamentally good and that social institutions corrupt it. The difficulty in accounting for how good creatures could create bad institutions is as evident in his *Discourse on the Origin of Inequality* as anywhere.

Michel Foucault and Jacques Derrida are among the most influential of very recent philosophers who insist that language uses us as much as we use language. Foucault's most forceful argument is found in *The Archeology of Knowledge*. The fundamentals of Derrida's position are laid out in his essay "Differance." In some of his works, Martin Heidegger, a twentieth-century German philosopher, elevates language to a more exalted status. Declaring that language is the "house of Being" he sometimes seems to think of the German language (along with Greek) as the palace of Being and of himself as its specially anointed caretaker. Such a posture can be found in his *Introduction to Metaphysics*. Be forewarned, however, that Heidegger's works, as well as Foucault's and Derrida's, can seem incomprehensible unless you have first read a lot of other philosophy.

5

Politics in the Face of Finitude: Review of Book VIII

ARISTOCRACY, TIMOCRACY, OLIGARCHY, AND TYRANNY REJECTED

If we accept Plato's implicit recognition of our finitude but reject his claim that finitude can finally be overcome through philosophy, what are our options? More specifically, what are our political options?

Tyranny, of course, is completely out of the question. To be under the thumb of someone who makes use of other persons and the resources of society to fulfill his or her own insatiable longing for completion and wholeness is, as Plato suggests, the worst political nightmare imaginable. But if, as I suggested in the last chapter, tyrants and Plato's philosophers seek to satisfy the same longing by different means, Plato's aristocratic city governed by philosopher-kings is also undesirable. If we reject the claim that philosophers can make contact with a singular, infinite, and eternal order of things, we will also reject the claim that society should be structured with the

119

primary aim of making it possible for philosophers to attain such knowledge.

Nor do most of us want to be ruled by military leaders in a timocracy. If living with limits means we have to rank the values we want to maximize and if we collectively rank values differently than do the members of other societies, then conflict between societies will sometimes reach the point where military leaders are needed. But few of us want to make into an end in itself the sort of honor Plato says is necessary to sustain soldiers in the heat of battle. To do so, as Plato shrewdly observes in his account of the character of timocracies, is to ask for more wars than are actually necessary, since the generals would always be stirring up trouble where it otherwise does not exist so as to have more battles in which to prove their honor (547e–548c).

We would likely mount a similar argument against rule by the rich. Wealth is a worthy value insofar as it allows us to enjoy other finite pleasures, but the pursuit of wealth for the sake of wealth is hollow and, perhaps, self-negating, as Plato argues in his account of the character of oligarchies and their decline into democracy (551c; 555b–557a). Unbridled pursuit of wealth, he contends, inevitably divides society into two warring camps, the rich and the poor. The rich, because they determine the rules of the game, get richer, and the poor get poorer. This ever-increasing polarization can continue for a while, but sooner or later the poor will successfully challenge the claim of the rich that they have a right to rule simply because they are rich. Plato's speculation that this opposition could take root in the trenches of the battlefield (556c–e), where the rich appear to the lean and hungry poor as overfed slobs who are no more fit for the task at hand than they are, even has some degree of historical accuracy.

DEMOCRACY BY DEFAULT

We seem to be left with democracy by default. That is not so bad, you might think, because, just as Plato contends, democracy seeks to maximize liberty and that is what we care about most. The beauty of democracy is that it is in fact the big tent Plato describes in Book VIII, under which all manner of persons are free to pursue whatever desires they like (557a–c). While Plato's ideal city excludes the pursuit of many desires, democracy makes room even for philosophers like himself to pursue their quest for the infinite and eternal.

But matters are more complicated than this. Plato argues that unbridled pursuit of liberty, like unrestrained pursuit of wealth, tends to negate itself. Too much of a good thing can lead to its opposite, and too much liberty can lead to slavery (563e–564a). Or consider Plato's remark that liberty in democracy can reach the point where even convicted criminals are free to roam the city (558a); this description, some would say, fits the state of affairs in many democracies today. It is a common view in the United States, for example, that we have gone so far in valuing liberty that we have made it difficult to convict criminals or keep them in jail long enough when we do manage to convict them. In the name of liberty, we have become prisoners in our own homes, afraid to venture into the streets after dark. This view overlooks the fact that only the former Soviet Union under Stalin and South Africa during apartheid imprisoned a higher percentage of its population than does the United States today. Nevertheless, you may believe that liberty has produced some of its opposite in other ways.

You might also find interesting Plato's argument that democracy can make people vulnerable to an even more pervasive enslavement, full-fledged tyranny. His account of how this might happen still focuses on wealth (564a–565d). Democracy throws the rich out as the sole governors, but since it permits pursuits of all kinds, some persons will continue to seek wealth, and the division of rich and poor continues. However, since the rich are not in sole control of the rules of the game any longer, the poor will often succeed in making laws that deprive the rich of their wealth. The rich can sometimes counteract such measures since they still have some input into making laws, but laws in general are unstable and render property very insecure.

The rich will protest that this is not fair, but power-hungry opportunists (and maybe even rich ones) will see a chance to make political hay and tell the poor that such protests are a sign that the rich are plotting a return to oligarchy, or conspiring against "the people." This challenge only inflames the rich even more; they struggle still harder to retain or recover their wealth and protest all the louder. This, in turn, is interpreted by the political opportunists as further evidence that there is a conspiracy afoot against democracy and the people. Finally, one of the opportunists promises to save the people from this conspiracy if only they give him the unlimited power to do so. The people agree, and tyranny is born.

Plato's account may focus too exclusively on wealth, but his description of the general dynamics that ensue when democracy frustrates a large segment of the population bears some similarity to modern accounts of the rise of tyrants. The rise of Napoleon Bonaparte in France, for example, loosely fits the general pattern outlined by Plato. One could also make a similar case for the rise of Hitler in Germany and Mussolini in Italy.

There is also more than a little resemblance between Plato's account and some strains of demagoguery in the United States. We have a long tradition, embodied in an array of theories, of seeing a giant conspiracy of "them" against "us." Who exactly "they" are varies from the Freemasons and a shadowy group known as the Illuminati in the eighteenth and nineteenth centuries, to the Trilateral Commission and the Business Round Table to the United Nations and a secret cabal of world bankers more often than not said to be controlled by Jews. While such conspiracy theories are often peddled by persons who are far from being poor, they seem to have the largest reception among persons who are looking for easy explanations and solutions for what they regard as their failure to enjoy the full benefits of democracy.

You might agree that Plato has some insights about the dangers lurking within democracy but argue that these problems do not constitute grounds for dismissing it, especially since we have no alternatives left. Although conspiracy theories abound in the United States, we have yet to erect a tyrant to protect us from the supposed conspirators that many people worry about. Furthermore, enough people still recognize, along with Plato, that liberty cannot be absolute, even in a democracy, that we have good reason to believe we can correct our excesses.

ANOTHER VIEW: PLATO AS A PROPONENT OF DEMOCRACY

Given the line of interpretation I have been pushing throughout this book, it may come as a surprise to learn that one school of commentators on the *Republic* argues that Plato was actually making a subtle argument in favor of democracy all along. These commentators agree that Plato never believed that his ideal city governed by philosopher-kings could actually be realized, a view I mentioned in chapter 4. They make the additional claim, however, that Plato believed we should not even strive to achieve the ideal city. In fact, they argue, this was Plato's central political message. The ideal city, they say, was constructed as a model of what we should never be tempted to try to put into practice. Thus, the *Republic* was intended as a lesson about the dangers of utopian politics.

This view may seem to turn Plato upside down, but it does help to make sense of some of Plato's more outrageous proposals. By this interpretation, for example, Plato's recommendation of the practice of eugenics and his prescription that property and even spouses should be held in common among the rulers, while absurd, are just the sort of radical measures that would have to be taken to establish the so-called ideal city. Such measures would be impossible to implement, and this is precisely Plato's point, these scholars argue. Indeed, the more absurd these measures are, and the more difficult they would be to implement — recall the recommendation to banish all persons over the age of twelve — the more effective Plato's warning against utopianism becomes. Proposals that strike most readers as utopian absurdities counting against Plato are transformed into prescient alarms rooted in hard-headed realism.

If Plato's real message in the *Republic* is to sound the alarm against utopianism, I can only applaud it. However, this interpretation has some severe problems. It entails some very strained and

contorted readings, and it makes highly selective use of some passages at the expense of others. But then all interpretations empha-
size the importance of some passages over others. A more important
problem with this interpretation is that it makes an incoherent
defense of democracy that has dangerous implications.

While the proponents of this view reject the more usual interpretation of Plato's political message, they tend to accept uncritically his
view of philosophy in general, and even much of its particular content. They seem to agree, for example, that the cosmos is through
and through a moral order; that philosophy can succeed in establish-
ing objective knowledge of this true nature of things, uncontami-
nated by the relativity of *nomos*; and that most persons are naturally
incapable of rising to this knowledge. The so-called ideal city governed by philosopher-kings is not utopian because philosophy is
incapable of achieving the aim Plato sets for it; rather, it is utopian
because in spite of the actual capabilities of philosophy, too many
people are skeptical of those capabilities, and their inevitable opposition to setting philosophers up as kings can be overcome only by
measures impossible to put into practice.

According to the prodemocracy reading of the *Republic*, Plato
himself realized that even useful lies would not be sufficient to overcome such opposition, and thus he opted for democracy; although it
would not put philosophers in power, it would at least allow them
the liberty to pursue contact with the infinite and eternal. The asym-
metry in Socrates' account of the perfectly unjust person and the
perfectly just person — the fact that he compares the happiness of a
tyrannical character, who is also tyrant in a tyrannical city, with the
happiness of a philosophic character, who lives not in an ideal city,
but in a corrupt one — is interpreted as Plato's way of stating that the
pursuit of philosophy is independent of politics. The same point is
seen in Plato's remarks that philosophers living in corrupt cities
might be better off to retreat from politics altogether (496d, 592a-b).

Insofar as democracy actually allows each of us to cultivate the
private garden of our own interests, I have no objection to drawing a
defense of democracy from Plato. And while I regard Plato's quest
for the infinite and eternal as futile, I am not calling for a political

regime that would deny the opportunity to those who wish to pursue it. But according to the prodemocracy interpretation, Plato's philosophers can retreat from politics and confidently enjoy the freedom provided by democracy even though democracy is supported only by the natural ignorance and moral stupidity of the rest of the population. Plato could hardly have been so dangerously naive. I doubt very much that he believed democracy can be sustained if the great majority of its participants lack an understanding of what it requires. Interpreting Plato as an up-front critic of democracy seems more plausible and coherent, and less dangerous, than seeing Plato as a closet-democrat defending democracy on antidemocratic presuppositions. While Plato saw that democracy could make room for persons like himself, he was also aware that it could easily produce a kind of tyranny that differs from the sort he describes in Book VIII, one in which a ruling majority tyrannizes over a minority that might include persons like himself.

APPROPRIATING PLATO'S CRITICISM
OF DEMOCRACY

If liberty must be restricted even in democracies, the question immediately arises: What liberties should be restricted and by whom? What other values will be upheld at the expense of liberty, and who will determine what those values are? Since liberty is always the liberty to do this or that in particular, if liberty is to be restricted, we have to determine who is going to decide which specific liberties are going to be restricted. These questions are certainly crucial, you might argue, but hardly pose a problem for democracy, since the answers to them define the very meaning of democracy.

We can simply follow the advice of Thomas Hobbes, whose theory of government was anticipated by Glaucon and Adeimantus in Book II of the *Republic*. Recall that Hobbes argued that if each of us pursues all our desires without limit, we will find ourselves in a war of all against all in which we will be able to fulfill very few, if any, of our desires. So we come to some agreement as to what kinds of behaviors will be allowed, or agree to appoint a special person or group of persons to make that determination, and agree to abide by it.

Of course, having chosen liberty as the most important value, we are not now going to backtrack by allowing any exclusive group of persons to decide how to limit liberty, whether this group is comprised of philosophers, generals, the rich, or persons of any other special sort. Since people differ in their beliefs about the things we should have the liberty to do, to allow the members of some exclusive group to make the choice would inevitably maximize their liberty at the expense of everyone else's. In a democracy we all participate in determining how we are going to restrict liberty.

True enough, but we must make sure we understand everything involved in going this route. While we may all participate in determining the things we will have the liberty to do, we will not all agree. It is because we recognize that people's beliefs differ in this regard that we give everyone a seat at the table in the first place. Democracy's answer to this problem, of course, is that to take a seat at the table is to agree to be bound by the will of the majority. But Hobbes's contention that the threat of the sword may be necessary to compel compliance to the social contract is no less true of democracy than of government by one or by an exclusive few. If a minority in a democracy forgets its agreement, the bottom line is that the majority will have to compel compliance by resorting to the threat of physical force.

This may seem obvious, but the ultimate consequences of democracy are often accepted all too cavalierly. As I noted in chapter 2, some of us embrace democracy because, unlike Plato, we are skeptical that there is a singular Truth woven into the cosmos that can tell us how we ought to conduct our lives. Others of us support democracy because, while we believe that there is such a Truth, we doubt that we have arrived at it and believe that allowing the freedom to explore various approaches to the Truth is the only way we will discover it. Yet others of us believe that there is such a Truth and that a few of us already know it, but that we do not have a right to impose it on others. In short, we all embrace liberty because we think it is the highest value.

Given that liberty is the supreme value, we should approach the task of restricting liberty with humility and great trepidation. While recognizing that the bottom line of democracy is obedience to the superior force of the majority, we should impose the will of the majority on the minority very cautiously, after much deliberation, and employ the threat of force only as a necessary last resort.

You might contend that this is just what we do. We are all familiar with the catechism, repeated in every introductory textbook on government, that democracy means majority rule with respect for minority rights. But think of the way in which we conduct our electoral politics. Plato once again may have his finger on the pulse of democracy as we generally practice it.

Consider the passage in Book VI (493a-c) where Plato is not addressing democracy directly but is clearly describing a situation he believes to be pervasive in democracies. Plato is contrasting sophists with what he regards as true philosophers. Sophists are skilled rhetoricians who, for a fee, concoct arguments in support of any opinion whatsoever. They also train people to argue in law courts. They have no concern for the truth and are interested only in devising persuasive speeches that serve the interests of those who hire them. The sophists, Socrates says, approach the public like they would a great beast. They are interested in discovering what makes it tick, but not for the purpose of redirecting its energies. They have no interest in true leadership, which means challenging people to question their conventional convictions and offering alternatives, but only articulate convictions that the great mass of people already have, for better or worse. Whatever it is that the people claim they desire and makes them happy the sophist calls good and just; and whatever it is that the people say vexes them the sophist calls bad and unjust.

For the sophists in this passage substitute today's political candidates and their intellectual guns for hire — the pollsters, consultants, and Madison Avenue marketing specialists who run campaigns — and you have a remarkably accurate portrayal of contemporary electoral politics. Rather than offering a great public debate in which candidates articulate alternative visions of the good life, election campaigns seem to simply mirror the majority thinking of the moment. Candidates often seem less interested in constructing new views about which way the public wagon ought to go than in making sure they are on the wagon with the biggest band. We can blame the candidates, but I suspect too many of us have also come to believe that "going with the flow" is all that elections are really about.

In much contemporary public discourse, the bottom line of democracy is too often made the first line. The majority, rather than making every attempt to accommodate dissenting views and then cautiously resigning itself to the fact that by benefit of numbers it has the final say, triumphantly announces that it is right and that it is right simply because it is the majority. How many times do we hear dissenting views condemned not by arguments against their substance but simply because they are outside the mainstream? In the classroom I often encounter students who, rather than providing arguments to support their opinions, assert that their opinion is good enough simply because it is theirs. "This is a democracy, and I have a right to my opinion," they say, implying that one opinion is as good as another, and that in adopting the principle of majority rule we make argument superfluous from the start. They seem to assume that the only relevant question is which opinion wins the largest show of hands. Like Thrasymachus, they imply that justice is simply obedience to the will of the strongest; and in a democracy the majority is the strongest. Such an attitude seems well on its way to supporting a tyranny of the majority over the minority. Plato, it seems, understood this weakness of democracy more than we might like to admit.

In the democracy of Athens, the highest offices of government were chosen by lot. We might pride ourselves on the fact that modern democracies do not use such an arbitrary means of selection. We might think that Plato was certainly right in rejecting democracy if that is what it means. However, our current democratic practices sometimes verge on being just as arbitrary in the way we affirm the will of the majority regardless of what it is.

DEMOCRACY AND PHILOSOPHY

You might protest that it is inconsistent of me to lament the sorry shape of public discourse and electoral politics when throughout this book I have said that I see no method of proving indisputably, and without circular reasoning, that one vision of the good life is superior to all others. If this is the case but we must nevertheless come to some collective agreement as to what we are going to permit and prohibit, why not forgo argument altogether? We could simply poll for the majority opinion, enforce it, and be done with politics. This approach, however, impoverishes democracy and does not necessarily follow from skepticism about proving the ultimate superiority of a given vision of the good life. Such skepticism should be directed toward even the views of the majority and calls for more, not less, critical scrutiny of them.

The most popular vision is sometimes nothing more than a jumbled collection of shifting, contradictory beliefs and whims. There is a difference between imposing such views without critical reflection and allowing a public debate in which people must act as philosophers of a sort to guide our policy. In the latter approach, people are called on to articulate clearly their view of life and at least some of its complexities, to state why they believe the pursuit of some values is better than others, and to trace the consequences of such a pursuit for other people and its impact on other values they consider to be important. A genuine public debate makes it possible for people to change their minds and discover that they have more in common with other people than they initially thought. The majority might even find it necessary to compel obedience less frequently than it would otherwise.

Of course, we cannot assume that if we all just get together, think hard, and talk for long enough, we will discover a complete harmony of interests. Somewhere or other we will reach certain rock-bottom differences on which somebody is going to have to give, voluntarily or otherwise. Nor can we assume that our irresolvable differences will only be minor ones, about which we can agree to disagree and go on our merry way. Situations may arise in which some persons find it necessary to disobey the law or even forcibly separate themselves from the government under which they live. To try to specify in advance of discussion precisely where people will draw a line in the sand amounts to giving up on the goal of living together, but democracy probably does have limits as to how much diversity it can accommodate. Democracy is not a magical panacea.

Even the limited hope I have for democracy, however, stems from my own particular view of our finite life and its complexities. I cannot step outside that view and demonstrate in any final way that other persons ought to take up my vision. I cannot trap people in a snare of moral logic. But I can listen to other people and try to find in their accounts of life some insights and experiences that resonate with my own. My experience leads me to believe that I have enough in common with enough other human beings to make mutual appreciation possible and philosophical discourse worthwhile.

Suggestions for Further Reading

The school of interpretation that argues the *Republic* is a subtle defense of democracy and a clever critique of utopianism originated with Leo Strauss; see *The City and Man*, chapter 2. Allen Bloom, a student of Strauss's, argues the same view in an interpretative essay appended to his translation of the *Republic*.

Many subsequent political thinkers have feared the potential in democracy for tyranny of the majority. In his *"Federalist Paper,"* no. 10, James Madison (the fourth president of the United States) praises the Constitution, which he had just helped to write, for the institutional restraints it places on the will of the majority. Alexis de Tocqueville, a French social theorist who toured the United States during the 1830s, wrote in his *Democracy in America* that Americans had fled the tyranny of monarchy and aristocracy only to come perilously close to falling into slavery to the whims of the majority. See especially book 4 of Richard Heffner's abridged edition. John Stuart Mill succinctly puts the threat of tyranny of the majority into historical context in *On Liberty*, chapter 1. He also addresses the issue in *Considerations on Representative Government*, especially chapters 5–7. Jose Ortega y Gasset, an early twentieth-century Spanish philosopher, offers a fascinating account in *The Revolt of the Masses* of how the very success of liberal democracy helps to produce what he calls "mass men," who believe that mediocrity is a positive good, that they need not submit their beliefs and values to the critical scrutiny of others, and that they have the right to impose there beliefs and values on everyone.

Select Bibliography

The following bibliography includes works I mention either in the main text or in the suggestions for further reading at the end of each chapter. Translations of Plato's works appear under the name of the translator.

Annas, Julia. *An Introduction to Plato's "Republic."* Oxford: Oxford University Press, Clarendon Press, 1981.

Aristophanes. *The Clouds.* Translated by Moses Hadas. In *The Complete Plays of Aristophanes.* Edited by Moses Hadas. New York: Bantam Books, 1962.

Aristotle. *Metaphysics.* Translated by Richard Hope. Ann Arbor, Mich.: University of Michigan Press, 1960.

Augustine. *The City of God.* Translated by Marcus Dods. New York: Random House, The Modern Library, 1950.

Bambrough, Renford, ed. *Plato, Popper and Politics.* Cambridge: W. Hefer and Sons, 1967.

——, ed. *New Essays on Plato and Aristotle.* London: Routledge and Kegan Paul, 1965.

Bloom, Allan, trans. *The "Republic" of Plato*. 2d ed. New York: Basic Books, 1968.

Burke, Edmund. *Reflections on the Revolution in France*. Buffalo, N.Y.: Prometheus, 1987.

Coole, Diana H. *Women in Political Theory: From Ancient Misogyny to Contemporary Feminism*. 2d ed. Boulder, Colo.: Lynne Rienner, 1993.

Cornford, Francis MacDonald, trans. *The "Republic" of Plato*. Oxford: Oxford University Press, 1941.

Cross, R. C., and A. D. Woozley. *Plato's "Republic": A Philosophical Commentary*. London: Macmillan, 1964.

Derrida, Jacques. "Differance." In *Speech and Phenomena: And Other Essays on Husserl's Theory of Signs*, translated by David B. Allison. Evanston, Ill.: Northwestern University Press, 1973.

Descartes, René. *Meditations on First Philosophy*. Translated by Donald A. Cress. Indianapolis, Ind.: Hackett, 1979.

Foucault, Michel. *The Archeology of Knowledge*. Translated by A. M. Sheridan Smith. New York: Pantheon, 1972.

Friedman, Milton. "The Future of Capitalism." Speech at Pepperdine University, Los Angeles, Calif., February 9, 1977. Reprinted in *Vital Speeches of the Day* 43 (March 1977): 333–37.

Goldman, Emma. *Anarchism and Other Essays*. Port Washington, N.Y.: Kennikat Press, 1969.

Grube, G. M. A., trans. *Plato: "Republic."* 2d ed. Revised by C. D. C. Reeve. Indianapolis, Ind.: Hackett, 1992.

———. *Plato's Thought*. Indianapolis, Ind.: Hackett, 1980.

Heidegger, Martin. *An Introduction to Metaphysics*. Translated by Ralph Manheim. New Haven, Conn.: Yale University Press, 1987.

Hobbes, Thomas. *Leviathan*. Edited by Michael Oakeshott. New York: Macmillan, Collier Books, 1962.

Hume, David. *A Treatise of Human Nature*. 2 vols. London: J. M. Dent and Sons, 1916. Reprint, London: Everyman's Library, 1968.

Jowett, Benjamin, trans. *The Dialogues of Plato*. Vol. 2. New York: Random House, 1937. Includes *Timaeus*, *Critas*, *Parmenides*, *Theatetus*, *Sophist*, *Statesman*, *Philebus*, and *Laws*.

————, trans. *The Best Known Works of Plato*. Garden City, N.Y.: Blue Ribbon Books, 1942. Includes *Republic, Symposium, Meno, Euthyphro, Apology, Crito*, and *Phaedo*.

Klosko, George. *The Development of Plato's Political Theory*. New York: Methuen, 1986.

Lee, H. D. P., trans. *Plato: The "Republic."* London: Penguin, 1956.

Locke, John. *An Essay Concerning Human Understanding*. 2 vols. Edited by Alexander Campbell Fraser. New York: Dover, 1959.

MacIntyre, Alasdair. *After Virtue*. Notre Dame, Ind.: Notre Dame Press, 1981.

Madison, James. "Federalist Paper" no. 10. In *The Federalist Papers*, edited by Willmore Kendall and George Carey. New Rochelle, N.Y.: Arlington House, 1966. The essay is also reprinted in many introductory textbooks on American government.

Marx, Karl. *Manifesto of the Communist Party*. In *The Marx-Engels Reader*, 2d ed., edited by Robert C. Tucker. New York: W. W. Norton, 1978.

————. *The German Ideology, Pt 1*. In *The Marx-Engles Reader*, 2d ed., edited by Robert C. Tucker. New York: W. W. Norton, 1978.

Mill, John Stuart. *Utilitarianism, On Liberty, and Considerations on Representative Government*. Edited by H. B. Acton. London: J. M. Dent and Sons, 1910. London: Everyman's Library, 1984.

Ortega y Gasset, Jose. *The Revolt of the Masses*. Translator anonymous. New York: W. W. Norton, 1957.

Pappas, Nickolas. *Plato and the "Republic."* New York: Routledge, 1995.

Popper, Karl. *The Open Society and Its Enemies*. Princeton, N.J.: Princeton University Press, 1950.

Reeve, C. D. C. *Philosopher-Kings: The Argument of Plato's "Republic."* Princeton, N.J.: Princeton University Press, 1988.

Rice, Daryl H. "Plato on Force: The Conflict between His Psychology and Political Sociology and His Definition of Temperance in the *Republic*." *History of Political Thought* 10 (1989): 565–76.

Rouse, W. H. D., trans. *Great Dialogues of Plato*. New York: New American Library, Mentor Books, 1956. Includes *Republic, Ion, Meno, Apology, Crito*, and *Phaedo*.

Rousseau, Jean-Jacques. *Discourse on the Origin of Inequality*. In *Rousseau: Basic Political Writings*, translated by Donald A. Cress. Indianapolis, Ind.: Hackett, 1987.

Sartre, Jean-Paul. *Nausea*. Translated by Lloyd Alexander. Norfolk, Conn.: New Directions Books, 1959.

Strauss, Leo. *The City and Man*. Chicago: Rand McNally, 1964.

Tocqueville, Alexis de. *Democracy in America*. Edited and abridged by Richard D. Heffner. New York: Penguin, New American Library, 1964.

Unamuno, Miquel de. *Tragic Sense of Life*. Translated by J. E. Crawford Flitch. New York: Dover, 1954.

Waterfield, Robin, trans. *Plato: "Republic."* Oxford: Oxford University Press, 1993.

Weber, Max. "Politics as a Vocation." In *From Max Weber: Essays in Sociology*, translated by H. H. Gerth and C. Wright Mills. New York: Oxford University Press, 1946.

Weinstein, Michael A. *Finite Perfections: Reflections on Virtue*. Amherst, Mass.: University of Massachusetts Press, 1985.

———. *Culture/Flesh*. Lanham, Md.: Rowman and Littlefield, 1995.

White, Nicholas P. *A Companion to Plato's "Republic."* Indianapolis, Ind.: Hackett, 1979.

Whitehead, Aflred North. *Adventures of Ideas*. New York: Free Press, 1967.

———. *Modes of Thought*. New York: Free Press, 1968.

———. *Process and Reality*. Corrected ed., Edited by David Ray Griffin and Donald W. Sherburne. New York: Free Press, 1978.

Wittgenstein, Ludwig. *Philosophical Investigations*. Translated by G. E. M. Anscombe. New York: Macmillan, 1953.

Vlastos, Gregory, ed. *Plato: A Collection of Critical Essays*. 2 vols. Garden City, N.Y.: Doubleday, Anchor Book, 1970–71. *Vol. 1, Metaphysics and Epistemology; Vol. 2, Ethics, Politics, and Philosophy of Art and Religion*.

Xenophon. *Memorabilia*. Translated by Amy L. Bonnette. Ithaca, N.Y.: Cornell University Press, 1994.

Zeitlin, Irving M. *Plato's Vision: The Classical Origins of Social and Political Thought*. Englewood Cliffs, N.J.: Prentice Hall, 1993.

Index

—ω—

Marx, K., 33
Mathematics
and certainty, 80
as ideal science, 71, 74–75
objects of, as kind of being,
68–70, 88
Metaphysics, 65–70, 83–90, 94,
98–100, 115. *See also*
Epistemology; Ontology
Mill, J. S., 64, 130
Moderation
in the city, 43–44, 56–57, 61, 64
in the soul, 60–61, 64, 104
Moralized cosmos, 22–26, 31, 124
Music, 45, 46. *See also* Art; Censorship
Myth
of Er, 116–17
of metals, 55–56, 108
and political legitimacy, 57
of shepherd and magical ring, 36

Narrative style, 46–49
Nature (*physis*)
Aristotle on, 66
as normative standard, 22–26,
31, 33, 39, 63, 83, 124
versus nurture, 42–44, 50,
54–55, 56, 57, 108, 113–14
and women, 54
Nominalism, 76–78, 88–89, 90
Nomos (custom; convention),
20, 22, 26, 31, 33, 81, 124
Nonbeing, 69, 86
Normative inquiry. *See* Empiri-
cal/normative distinction

Oligarchic man, 94–96, 105, 106
Oligarchy, 94–96, 105
Ontology, 65–70. *See also* Being,
kinds of
Order, 85, 95–96, 103–4
Ordinary objects as type of
being, 68–70, 79–80, 86–88
Ortega y Gasset, J., 130
Overseers (rulers), 41–44,
61–63. *See also* Philoso-
phers, as overseers

Pain, 99, 115
Painting, 68, 80, 82. *See also*
Art; Censorship
Pappas, N., 32, 90
Particulars, participation of, in
forms, 75–78, 79. *See also*
Universals
Petitio principii (begging the
question), 88–89
Philosopher-kings. *See* Philosophers, as overseers
Philosophers
education of 70–74, 80
as judges of highest pleasure,
98–100
as overseers (rulers), 42–44,
58–63, 108–10, 113–14,
119, 123–25
Philosophy
and appearance and reality,
8–11, 31, 38, 65–66, 85–86,
99–100, 105
and appetites, 102–4
and art, 49, 80, 101–2, 115–16